guide to Granada

Text, photographs, design, lay-out and printing, entirely created by the technical department of EDITORIAL ESCUDO DE ORO, S.A.

Palaudarias, 26 - 08004 Barcelona (Spain).

e-mail:editorial@eoro.com
http://www.eoro.com

2nd Edition

I.S.B.N. 84-378-1906-7

Dep. Legal B. 29823-2000

Editorial Escudo de Oro, S.A.

THE VISIT TO GRANADA

Visitors have always given Granada the highest praise, reaching the unanimous opinion that it ranks amongst the most beautiful cities in the world. Indeed, this is a city of incomparable monumental wealth, exquisite parks and gardens, hospitable people and rich history, combined with a splendid geographical situation in which it rises majestic between the Mediterranean Sea and the peaks of the Sierra Nevada, landscapes which confer a magical luminosity on the city of Granada.

All these elements combine to make Granada a unique, different city whose complexity makes it necessary to allow ample time to get to know it. For Granada has been an important centre since ancient times, and many civilisations and cultures have passed through, leaving their mark on the city and its development. It is a city full of contrasts, where deeply-rooted traditions survive amidst the hustle and bustle of modern-day life, where much of its Moorish past lives side-by-side with elements of more recent history. It is, moreover, and always has been, a friendly, welcoming city.

This guide aims to be the perfect travelling companion on this visit to Granada. Five itineraries embrace all the most important sights in the city, each of them accompanied by a map. There is also a complete map of the city on pages 8 and 9. The guide is completed by sections on the history, gastronomy, festivities and arts and crafts of Granada, with a final chapter devoted to Granada province, describing various excursions which can be made from the capital.

The Patio de los Leones («Courtyard of the Lions»), universally known symbol of the Alhambra and maximum splendour of Nasrite art.

The Albaicín district, the original urban nucleus of Granada.

HISTORICAL INTRODUCTION

Evidence has been found proving that Granada's Albaicín Hill has been settled since the Bronze Age. The people of this early settlement later entered into contact with Phoenicians, Greeks and Carthaginians, particularly in the seafaring areas of the province. The Iberian city founded on the Albaicín, known as Ilbyr or *Elibyrge,* a name which later became *Ilíberis,* acquired importance during Roman times when it was granted the status of municipality in around 27 BC and given the name of *Municipium Florentium Iliberritanum,* becoming one of the principal urban nuclei in the region. An outstanding figure in the introduction of Christianity to Granada was Saint Cecil, the city's first bishop, martyred here. During this new period, the religious importance of *Ilíberis* is shown by the fact that it was chosen in 313 to host the first Church Council in Spain.
When in the year 711 Tariq's forces landed on the Peninsula, the

strength of the reigning Visigoth monarchy was being undermined by internal strife. Three years later, the Moors reached Granada, soon conquering the entire region. There was already a Jewish population living outside the walls of ancient *Ilíberis,* on the other side of the River Darro and at the foot of the Torres Bermejas. This settlement was known as *Garnata al Yahud,* and it is from this that the present name of the city derives.

During the almost eight centuries of Moorish domination, Granada's fortunes took many turns, for better and for worse. During the Emirate of Cordoba, it was capital of the Granadan territories, that is, the lands bordering the Sierra Elvira, until Zawi Zirí converted them into his kingdom in 1013. Under the Ziries, Granada became a flourishing city. Walls were built all around it and the palace-fortress ofss Alcazaba Cadima was raised in the centre of the Albaicín. The Ziries were succeeded in power by the Almoravides (1090) and the Almohades (1190). In 1238, the Kingdom of Granada was created as a result of the disintegration of the Almohade empire and the advances of the Christian armies. This new state was proclaimed by Mohammed Ibn al-Ahmar, Emir of Arjona and founder of the Nasrite dynasty, thanks to truces signed with the Christians and the support of his allies the Marinies in the Maghreb. All this helped to cement the foundations of a solid reign, though

A painting representing the ten first Nasrite kings in conversation (Sala de los Reyes, in the Alhambra).

"The Surrender of Granada", reproduction by Moreno Carbonero. (Chapel Royal).

the peace was always precarious due to the constant pressure of the Christians and internal conflicts. The kingdom stretched from Murcia to Gibraltar, and over the next two-and-a-half centuries Granada was the last remaining bastion of Islam in the West.

Under Yusuf I, who ascended to the throne in 1333, and his son, Mohammed V, the Kingdom of Granada enjoyed its period of maximum splendour. The peace which reigned thanks to truces agreed with Castile and the Maghreb permitted real cultural and economic development, and steady, important trade links were set up with both the West and the East. In its turn, La Madraza, the Islamic university founded by Yusuf I, became the principal cultural centre in Granada. The Nasrite palaces in the Alhambra, built by Yusuf and his son, are the most magnificent exponents of this splendid period.

Internal conflict, economic problems and Christian pressure finally led to the surrender of Granada in 1492, when Boabdil, the last Nasrite king, handed over the city to the Catholic Monarchs. The treaties of surrender signed between the two sides stipulated that there should be respect for the language, faith and customs of the defeated Moors, but their conversion to Christianity was soon decreed, with expulsion the only alternative. Moors accepting this imposition were known as Moriscos, and their continual suppression led many to rise up against the new power centre, often taking refuge in the Alpujarra region, until the order for complete expulsion was given in 1611.

After the Christian reconquest, much of the city's physiognomy underwent change, with the construction of churches and palaces in the Renaissance style. Granada's destiny was now linked to that of the rest of Spain, and it lived through many more important chapters of history. One of the most outstanding events since the reconquest was the uprising against the Napoleonic army, which had as its consequence the execution of the young local heroine Mariana Pineda in 1831. In recent years, social, political and economic dynamism have combined to promote the industrial and commercial expansion of the city, which has become established as the capital of Eastern Andalusia. Culture, too, has continued to play a strong part in the development of Granada, and to its outstanding historic and artistic heritage have been added such recent creations as the Science Park and the staging of theatre, music and dance festivals of enormous international prestige.

Paseo del Salón

Cerca de Don Gonzalo
HAZA GRANDE
Puerta de Fajalauza
CUEVAS COLORADAS
PLTA. M. CANASTERA
LA RAUDA
SACROMONTE
Palacio los Córdo
Casa del Chapiz
CALLEJON DEL BOLI
PESO DE LA HARINA
CTA. CHAPIZ
CUESTA VEREDILLA
ALBAICIN
PLTA. CRUZ DE PIEDRA
CRUZ DE PIEDRA
CARRIL DE S. MIGUEL
PL. LUQUE
SAN GREGORIO
CALLEJON DE LA ALBERZANA
PLAZOLETA DEL ABAD
San Salvador
Conv. Sto. Tomás
CARRIL TOMASAS
S. Juan de los Reyes
Museo Arqueológico
Conv. Sta. Catalina de Zafra
Mirador San Nicolas
PL. SAN NICOLAS
PL. LARGA
PLTA. NUEVA
ARCO PESAS
PLTA. ALMONA
PLTA. MINAS
PL. CARNICEROS
PLTA. SAN BARTOLOME
MURCIA
I. E. M.
Mirador de S. Cristobal
PLTA. SAN CRISTOBAL
SAN ANTONIO
Muralla de la Alcazaba
Pal. Dar Al Horra
Convento de Sta. Isabel la Real
S. Miguel Bajo
PL. GALLO
Puerta Monaita
Baños Arabes
Casa de los Pisa
CUESTA SAN CRISTOBAL
CARRIL DE LA LONA
CRUZ DE QUIROS
Iglesia de San Ildefonso
Gobierno Militar
La Merced
ACERA DE SAN ILDEFONSO
PLAZA DEL TRIUNFO
Puerta Elvira
Hospital Real
PLAZA LIBERTAD
CARRETERA DEL ... ELVIRA
GRAN VIA DE COLON
Monasterio Sta. Paula
Fuente del Triunfo
Jardines del Triunfo
AVENIDA DEL HOSPICIO
Delg. Hacienda
CONSTITUCION
SAN JUAN DE DIOS
Convento Encarnación
Stos. Justo y Pastor
PLAZA UNIVERSIDAD
Universidad
Jardín Botánico
Iglesia y Hospital de S. Juan de Dios
Iglesia del Perpetuo Socorro
Real Monasterio San Jerónimo
PLAZA TRINIDAD
PLAZA ROMANILLA
DUQUESA
CATE

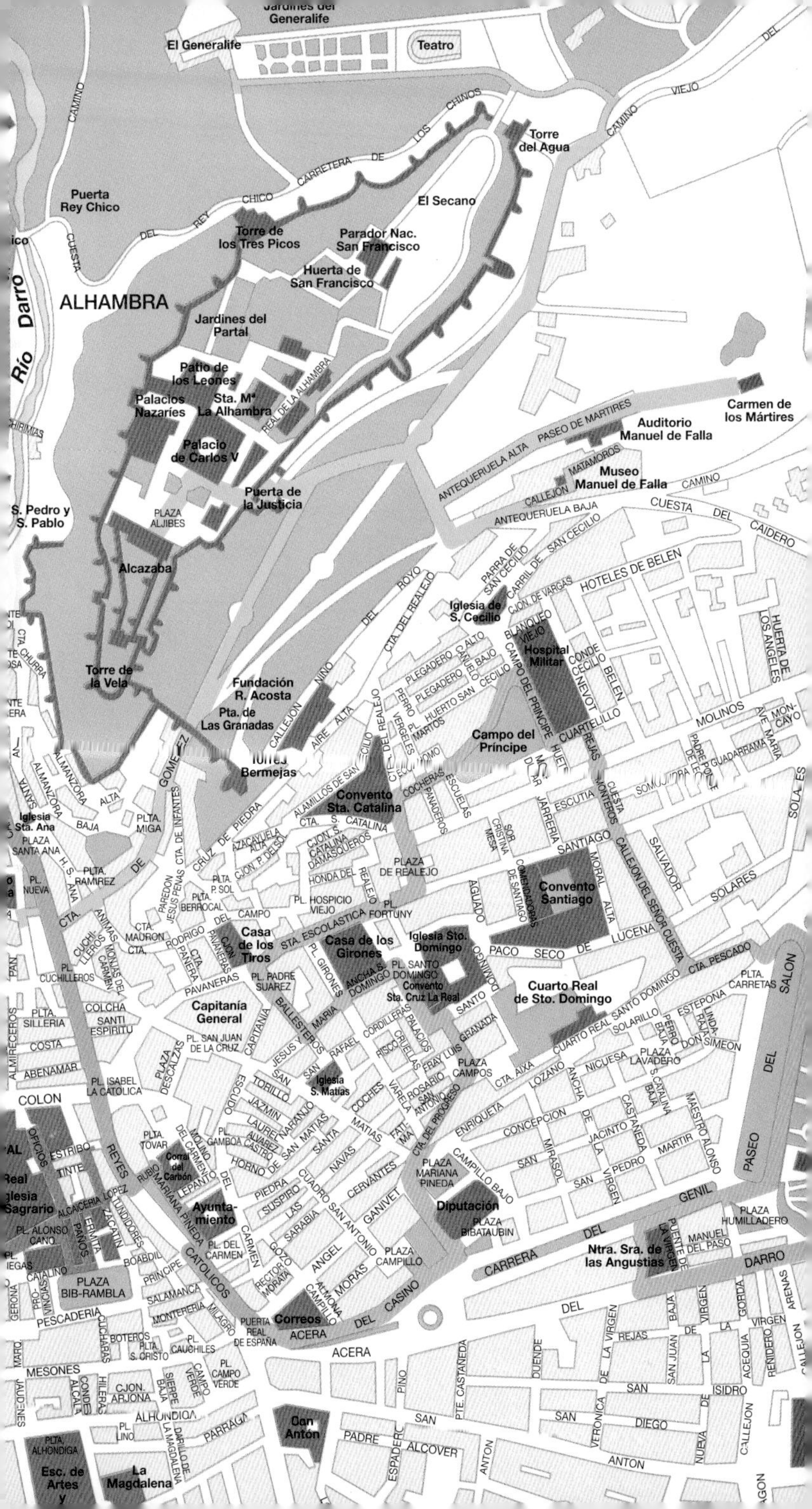

Jardines del Generalife
El Generalife
Teatro
CAMINO VIEJO DEL
CARRETERA DE LOS CHINOS
Torre del Agua
Puerta Rey Chico
CUESTA DEL REY CHICO
Torre de los Tres Picos
El Secano
Parador Nac. San Francisco
Huerta de San Francisco
ALHAMBRA
Río Darro
Jardines del Partal
Patio de los Leones
Palacios Nazaríes
Sta. Mª La Alhambra
REAL DE LA ALHAMBRA
Palacio de Carlos V
Puerta de la Justicia
PLAZA ALJIBES
S. Pedro y S. Pablo
Alcazaba
Torre de la Vela
CHIRIMIAS
CTA. CHURRA
Carmen de los Mártires
Auditorio Manuel de Falla
PASEO DE MARTIRES
ANTEQUERUELA ALTA
MATAMOROS
Museo Manuel de Falla
CALLEJON
CAMINO
ANTEQUERUELA BAJA
CUESTA DEL CAIDERO
PARRA DE SAN CECILIO
CARRIL DE SAN CECILIO
HOTELES DE BELEN
CJON. DE VARGAS
Iglesia de S. Cecilio
BLANQUEO VIEJO
Hospital Militar
HUERTA DE LOS ANGELES
CTA. DEL REALEJO
NIÑO DEL ROYO
Fundación R. Acosta
Pta. de Las Granadas
Torres Bermejas
CALLEJON
AIRE ALTA
PLEGADERO ALTO
PLEGADERO BAJO
CANDIL
HUERTO SAN CECILIO
PERRO
VERGELES
PL. MARTOS
CAMPO DEL PRINCIPE
CONDE CECILIO
NEVOT
BELEN
CUARTELILLO
MOLINOS
AVE MARIA
MONCAYO
Campo del Príncipe
GUADARRAMA
PADRE POVEDA
SOMOSIERRA
SOLARES
ALMANZORA ALTA
ALMANZORA BAJA
GOMEREZ
CTA. DE INFANTES
Iglesia Sta. Ana
PLAZA SANTA ANA
PLTA. MIGA
CRUZ DE PIEDRA
ALAMILLOS DE SAN CECILIO
Convento Sta. Catalina
CTA. S. CATALINA
COCHERAS
PANADEROS
ESCUELAS
SOR CRISTINA MESA
JARRERIA
ESCUTIA
CUESTA
MONTEROS
REJAS
SALVADOR
AZACAYUELA ALTA
CJON. P. DEL SOL
CJON. S. CATALINA
DAMASQUEROS
PLAZA DE REALEJO
SANTIAGO
MORAL ALTA
CALLEJON DEL SEÑOR CUESTA
H. S. ANA
PLTA. RAMIREZ
PL. NUEVA
PAREDON
JESUS PEÑAS
PLTA. P. SOL
PLTA. BERROCAL
HONDA DEL REALEJO
PL. HOSPICIO VIEJO
PL. FORTUNY
AGUADO
COMENDADORAS DE SANTIAGO
Convento Santiago
CTA.
ANIMAS
CUCHILLEROS
CTA. MAURON
RODRIGO DEL CAMPO
Casa de los Tiros
STA. ESCOLASTICA
Casa de los Girones
Iglesia Sto. Domingo
PACO SECO DE LUCENA
CTA. PESCADO
SALON
PL. CUCHILLEROS
MONJAS DEL CARMEN
CTA. PANERA
CJON. PAVANERAS
PAVANERAS
PL. PADRE SUAREZ
PL. GIRONES
ANCHA S. DOMINGO
PL. SANTO DOMINGO
Convento Sta. Cruz La Real
DOMINGO
Cuarto Real de Sto. Domingo
PLTA. CARRETAS
PLTA. SILLERIA
COLCHA
SANTI ESPIRITU
Capitanía General
CAPITANIA
BALLESTEROS
MARIA
JESUS Y MARIA
SANTO
GRANADA
CUARTO REAL SANTO DOMINGO
SOLARILLO
ESTEPONA
LINDARAJA
DON SIMEON
PERRO BAJA
PLAZA LAVADERO
COSTA
PL. SAN JUAN DE LA CRUZ
PLAZA DESCALZAS
RAFAEL
CORDILLERAS
PALACIOS
RISCO
CRUELLAS
FRAY LUIS
PLAZA CAMPOS
CTA. AIXA
LOZANO
NICUESA
ANCHA DE CASTAÑEDA
S. CATALINA BAJA
MAESTRO ALONSO
PASEO DEL SALON
ALMIRECEROS
ABENAMAR
PL. ISABEL LA CATOLICA
ESCUDO
TORILLO
SAN
Iglesia S. Matías
COCHES
VARELA
ROSARIO
SAN ANTONIO
COLON
JAZMIN
LAUREL
NARANJO
SAN MATIAS
MATIAS
FATIMA
CTA. DEL PROGRESO
ENRIQUETA
CONCEPCION
JACINTO
MIRASOL
SAN PEDRO MARTIR
DE LA VIRGEN
OFICIOS
ESTRIBO
TINTE
REYES
PLTA. TOVAR
RUBIO
PL. GAMBOA
ALVAREZ CASTRO
MOLINO DEL CARMEN
Corral del Carbón
MARIANA PINEDA
LEPANTO
DEL
HORNO DE SANTA
NAVAS
CERVANTES
PLAZA MARIANA PINEDA
CAMPILLO BAJO
SAN
Real
Iglesia Sagrario
ALCAICERIA
LOPEZ
ZACATIN
PL. ALONSO CANO
ERMITA
PAÑOS
TUNDIDORES
Ayuntamiento
PIEDRA
SUSPIRO
LAS
CUADRO
SARABIA
GANIVET
Diputación
PLAZA BIBATAUBIN
GENIL
PLAZA HUMILLADERO
PUENTE DE LA VIRGEN
MANUEL DEL PASO
Ntra. Sra. de las Angustias
CARRERA DEL DARRO
PL. DEL CARMEN
CARMEN
CATOLICOS
BOABDIL
PRINCIPE
CATALINO
PL. VIEGAS
PLAZA BIB-RAMBLA
GERONA
PRO-VINCIAS
SALAMANCA
MONTERERIA
MILAGRO
GOZO
RECTOR MORATA
ANGEL
ALMONA CAMPILLO
MORAS
PLAZA CAMPILLO
CASINO
DEL
PESCADERIA
CUCHARAS
BOTEROS
PLTA. S. CRISTO
PL. CAUCHILES
PUERTA REAL DE ESPAÑA
Correos
ACERA DEL CASINO
ACERA
REJAS
DEL
SAN JUAN
BAJA
VIRGEN DE LA
GORDA
ARENAS
VIRGEN
ACEQUIA
RENIDERO
CALLEJON
MARQ.
MESONES
JAUDENES
CONDES ALCALA
HILERAS
CJON. ARJONA
SIERPE BAJA
CAMPO VERDE
PL. CAMPO VERDE
ALHONDIGA
PL. LINO
LA MAGDALENA
DARILLO DE LA MAGDALENA
PARRAGA
San Antón
PINO
PTE. CASTAÑEDA
DUENDE
SAN
ISIDRO
VERONICA
NUEVA DE SAN ANTON
PADRE ALCOVER
ESPADERO
ANTON
SAN DIEGO
SAN ANTON
CALLEJON
PLTA. ALHONDIGA
Esc. de Artes y
La Magdalena

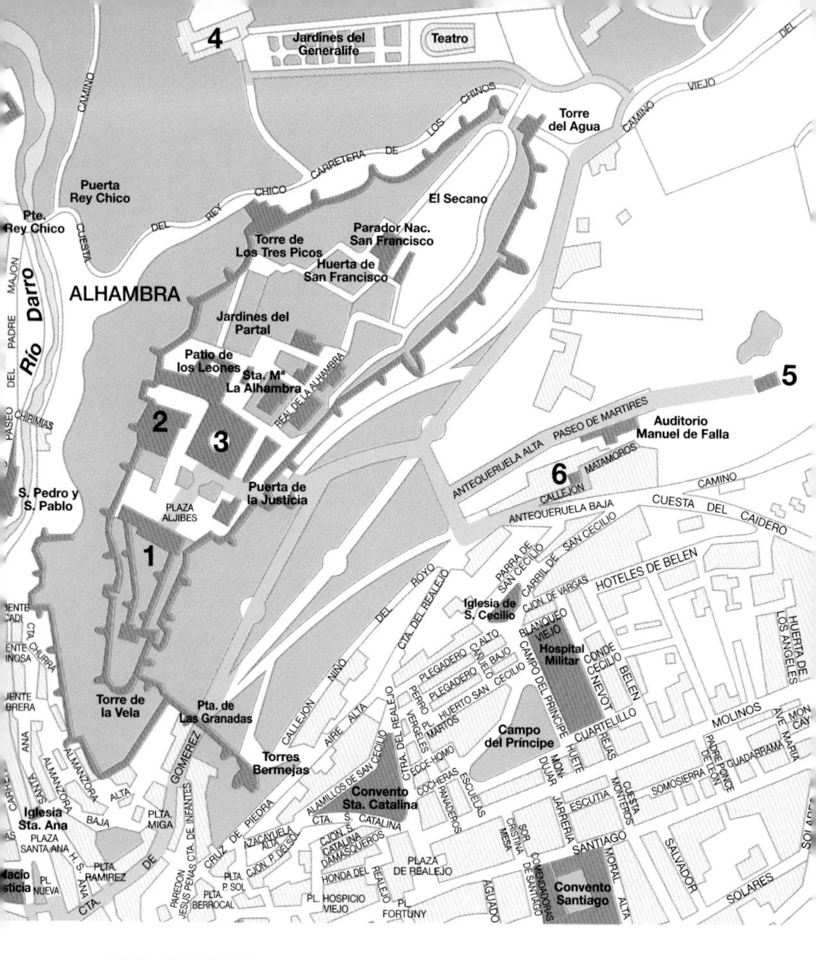

THE ALHAMBRA

1. Alcazaba
2. Nasrite Palaces
3. Palace of Carlos V and Alhambra and Fine Arts Museums
4. Generalife
5. Carmen de los Mártires
6. Manuel de Falla House-Museum.

Starting in Plaza Nueva, we climb up Cuesta de Gomérez, contemplating, before we enter the walled enclosure, a final vision of the exterior, which gives us the image of such an austere structure that it is is impossible to imagine the marvels we shall find inside. Its name is derived from an Arabic word meaning «red castle», in allusion to the reddish colour of the materials used in its construction, though Moorish historian

and poet Ibn al Jatib attributes it to the fact that the fortress was built at night, by torchlight.
On *Sabika* hill, as it was known to the Moors, where the Alcazaba now stands, there was once a Visigoth fortress, parts of which were used by the Muslim conquerors. In the 11th century, the Ziries reformed the castle, building a wall linking it to the Albaicín and thus integrating it into the walled part of the city. Later, Mohammed I, founder of the Nasrite dynasty, established his residence on the hill for greater security, building the present Alcazaba and beginning the construction of a palace and walls. The principal elements in the Alhambra are the work of Yusuf I (1333-1354) and his son, Mohammed V (1354-1391). After the Christian reconquest, the Catholic Monarchs carried out some alterations and Charles V later built the Renaissance palace which bears his name.
At the end of Cuesta de Gomérez, beyond the doorway of the **Puerta de las Granadas** stretch before us the **Alamedas of the Alhambra,** a leafy wood landscaped in the 16th century and formerly occupied by defensive elements. A path rises up, leading to the main entrance, the **Puerta de la Justicia.** This is the most monumental doorway in the Alcazaba, featuring a great Moorish arch built in the time of Yusuf I. Next to it is the **Pilar de Carlos V,** a lovely Renaissance fountain designed by Pedro Machuca in

View of the Alhambra from Paseo de los Tristes.

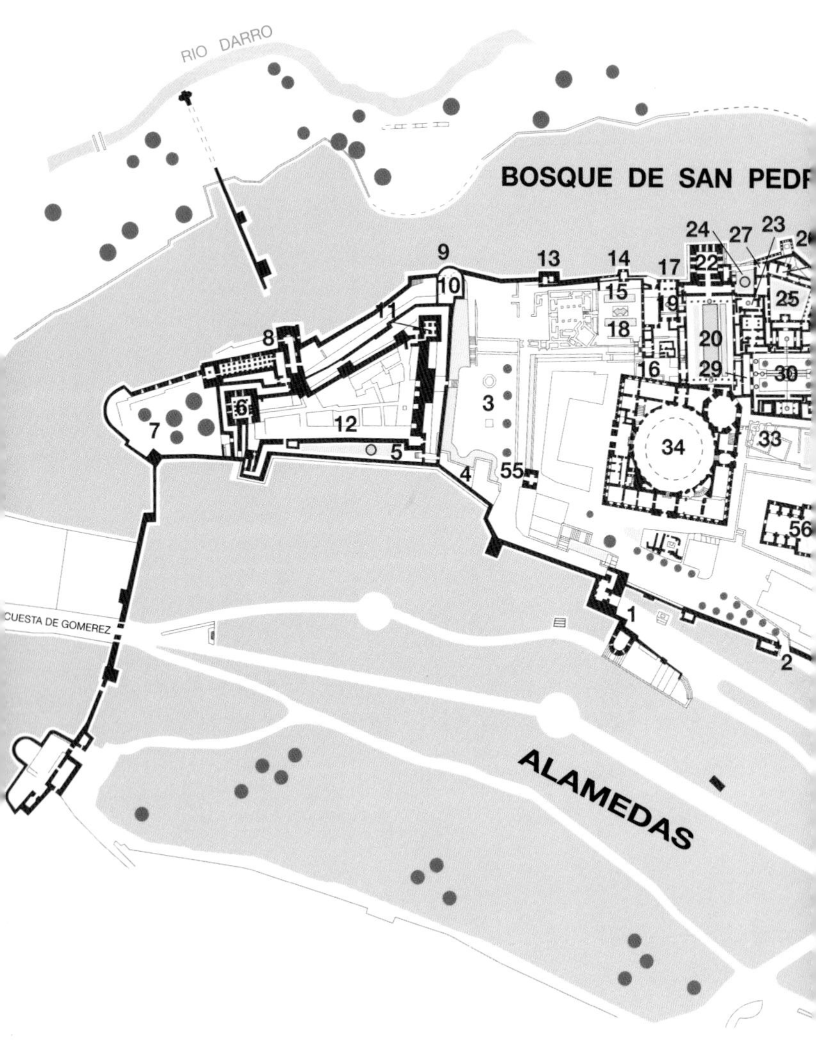

A. Door of Los Gomerez (entrance to the Alhambra).
1. Door of La Justicia (pedestrian entrance).
2. Door of El Carril (vehicle entrance).
3. Plaza de los Aljibes.
4. Entrance to the Alcazaba.
5. Garden of Los Adarves.
6. Tower of La Vela.
7. Battlements.
8. Towerand Gate of Las Armas.
9. Torre Redonda.
10. Keep.
11. Torre Quebrada.
12. Parade ground.
13. Torre of Mohamed.
14. Tower of Machuca.
15. Patio of Machuca.
16. Entrance to the Palacio Real.
17. Oratory.
18. Mexuar Patio.
19. Cuarto Dorado («Gold Room») or de las Flechas («of the Arrows»).
20. Patio of Comares.
21. Sala de la Barca.
22. Comares Tower.
23. Baths.
24. Patio of Los Cypreses.
25. Garden of Lindaraxa.
26. Tower of Abul Hachach.
27. Apartments of Charles V.
28. Sala de las Frutas.
29. Harem of the Sala de Los Leones.
30. Patio of Los Leones.

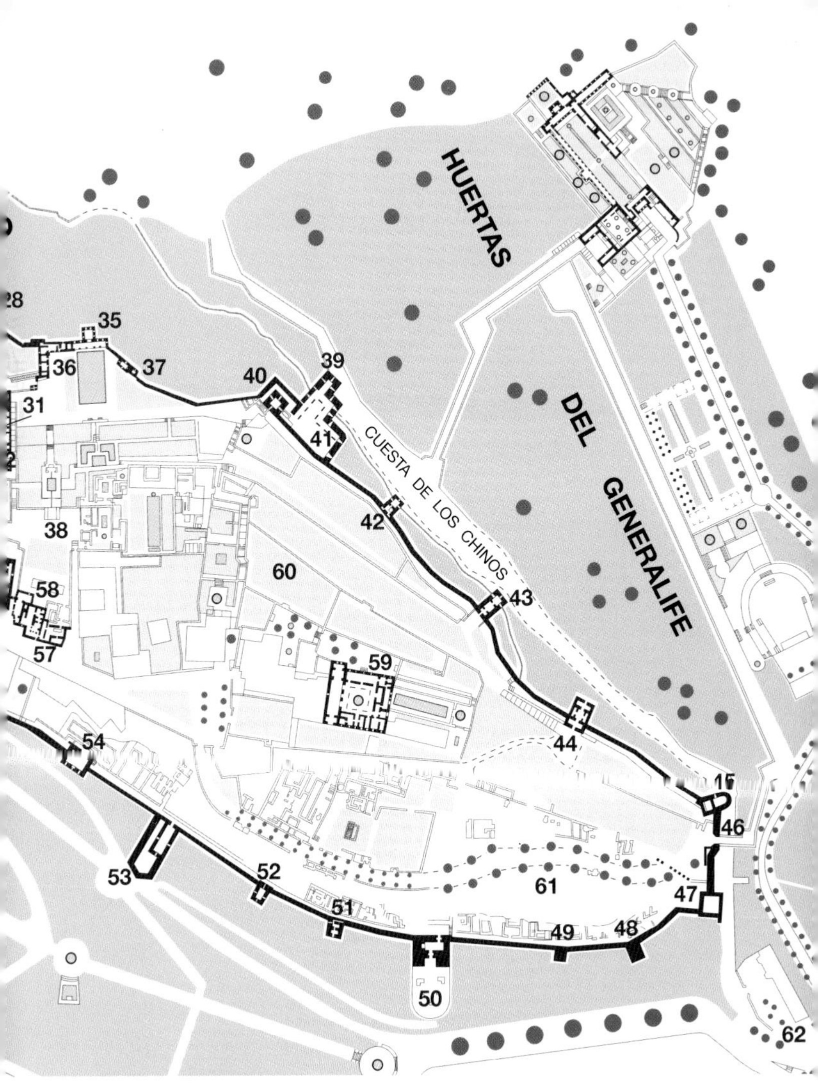

31. Sala de los Reyes.
32. Tower of the Rauda.
33. Rauda (royal cemetery).
34. Palace of Charles V.
35. Tower of Las Damas.
36. Moorish houses.
37. Tower of the Mihrab.
38. Gardens of El Partal.
39. Tower of Los Picos.
40. Door of El Arrabal.
41. Battlements.
42. Tower of El Cadi.
43. Tower of La Cautiva.
44. Tower of Las Infantas.
45. Tower of El Cabo de la Carrera.
46. Aqueduct.
47. Tower of El Agua.
48. Tower of Juan de Arce.
49. Tower of Baltasar de la Cruz.
50. Tower and Gate of the Siete Suelos.
51. Tower of El Capitán.
52. Watchtower.
53. Tower of Las Cabezas.
54. Tower of Peralada.
55. Door of El Vino.
56. Church of Santa María de la Alhambra.
57. Calle Real or Calle Mayor.
58. Moorish Baths.
59. *Parador* (state hotel) of San Francisco.
60. Gardens of San Francisco.
61. Gardens of El Secano.
62. Ticket office. Parking.

Pillar of Carlos V and Puerta de la Justicia («Justice Gate»).

austere Bramantesque style and whose spouts represent the three rivers of Granada: the Beyro, the Darro and the Genil.
Through the Puerta de la Justicia with its zigzagging structure we now come to an esplanade facing the Palace of Carlos V, which now serves as the starting-point of visits to the site. At one end, delimiting the zone of palaces and the Medina, is the **Puerta del Vino** («Wine Gate»), leading to the **Plaza de los Aljibes,** the antechamber to the Alcazaba. The lintel of the inner façade of the Puerta del Vino features a symbolic key and an inscription in praise of Allah and Mohammed V.
The **Alcazaba (1)** stands at the highest point on the hill, surrounded by thick walls and a number of towers which enclose a site known as the Barrio Castrense. Here we find the ruins of old houses, dungeons, a cistern and baths. The entire defensive system of the Alhambra was controlled from the Keep, as this commanded a view of practically the entire surrounding area up to the Torre del Agua at the other end of the walled enclosure,

as well as allowing vigilance of the Torre de las Armas and the Puerta de las Armas, the entrance from the Albaicín. The tower known as the Torre de la Pólvora, for its part, controlled access from the Cuesta de Gomérez, whilst the Torre de la Vela dominated the entire city. This last tower is also known as the Torre de la Campana, the Catholic Monarchs having installed a bell in it to ring out irrigation times on the surrounding plains. The Torre de la Vela commands views of the 11th-century **Torres Bermejas.** These formed a small independent castle, joined to the Alhambra by the wall, completing the defensive system on the Mauror hill, site of the old Jewish quarter.
Whilst the Alcazaba, an eminently military zone, surprises due to its austerity, the **Nasrite palaces (2)** astound us due to their rich and exquisite ornamental qualities, so characteristic of Nasrite art. «Nasrite art» is the name given to artistic manifestations during the existence of the Kingdom of Granada, when conditions of independence allowed the development of highly particular forms. These feature obviously Western influences, such as the exceptional presence of representations of animate forms, prohibited by the Koran, but their main characteristic is their enormous decorative richness. In the Alhambra, this art

The Alhambra from the Torre de la Vela.

The Mexuar Patio and Comares Front.

touches the sublime, and all its rooms, courtyards and gardens partake of a refined, poetic atmosphere.
The palace complex can be divided into two main areas: the **Palacio de Comares** (built by Yusuf I) and the **Palacio de los Leones** (by Mohammed V). These palaces are organised in accordance with the typical Oriental layout, that is, with different official and private apartments, and baths, all arranged around a large courtyard, or patio. Our visit begins in the Palacio de Comares, in the area known as the Mexuar, now much-altered from its original appearance by many later reforms and additions, such as coats of arms and other Castilian symbols. A small patio gives access to the **Sala del Mexuar,** where the council of viziers or ministers met. At the rear is the **Oratory,** which conserves a small *mihrab.* Next, we come to the **Cuarto Dorado** («Golden Room»), built under Mohammed V and which, like the previous room, commands splendid views over the Albaicín. The Cuarto Dorado leads into the **Patio del Mexuar,**

which has a washing fountain and features the so-called Comares Façade, one of the finest examples of Nasrite art.
The most outstanding element is a magnificent frieze of *alicatado* (arrangements of glazed tiles) and complex stucco decoration. The ornamental motifs reproduced in theses Arabesques are floral («ataurique») or purely linear and geometrical («lazo»), as well as various epigraphic texts, so harmoniously blended with the rest of the decoration that the untrained eye will often fail to recognise them. Some of these are religious texts, others poems. Some are in Kufic script (a more angular style), others in cursive or *nasjí* letters. One phrase is constant in all the rooms: «*La gallib illa Allah*» («There is no victor but God»). The colours, now much faded, are gold, symbolising royalty, red (power), green (paradise) and blue (the hope of attaining paradise). Also striking is the contrast between the rich interior decoration and the austerity of the exterior. This responds to the idea that in inner life, that is, spirituality and the family, lies true wealth.

The Patio of Los Arrayanes («Courtyard of the Myrtles).

The Salón de Embajadores («Audience Chamber»).

We now pass into the **Patio de los Arrayanes** («Courtyard of the Myrtles»), the centre of the Palace of Comares. It will be noted that we have entered this courtyard from one end, so that our first view of it is oblique, making it appear much larger than it actually is. The patios are so arranged as to receive sunlight throughout the day. The courtyard and the garden were vital spaces for the Moors, and the place where that fundamental element, water, flows. But water is, above all, a crucial ornamental element in the Nasrite Palaces. Water reflects both the architecture and nature, and gives freshness and colour. A carefully-designed system of water spouts and fountains ensures that the water forms only the slightest ripple on its emergence, both to conserve its function as a mirror and to ensure that its sounds do not make a distracting noise, but harmonious, restful music.
The north gallery of the Patio of the Myrtles gives entry to the **Sala de la Barca,** or of the *Baraka* («blessing» in Arabic), antechamber to the **Salón de Embajadores** (Audience Cham-

ber), which occupies the ground floor of the majestic Torre de Comares. This tower, with a height of 45 metres, is the highest tower in the Alhambra. We are now in the most beautiful of all the rooms in the Alhambra. Everything here is profusely decorated, with not one square centimetre exempt from rich artistic adornment. The very walls are like an open book, featuring over 300 religious phrases, as well as the motto of the Nasrite dynasty. The Sala de la Barca is square in shape, each side measuring 11.3 metres, with a height of 18.2 metres. Nine balconies, forming small rooms, open off from the walls, giving onto the exterior through windows of coloured glas. These are the so-called *comarías* which give this palace its name. In the middle of the room is conserved part of the original floor, of glazed ceramic. The ceiling, for its part, is another masterpiece of Nasrite carpentry, representing the seven heavens of the Muslim paradise, culminating in the eighth, where Allah lives.
The east side of the Courtyard of the Myrtles leads to the **Palacio de los Leones,** formerly independent of the Palacio de Comares. The centre of the palace is the **Patio de los Leones** («Courtyard of the Lions»), in its day a garden chronicles likened to paradise. The patio is encircled by 124 fine

Patio de los Leones.

Dome of mocarabs in the Abencerrajes Room.

white marble columns as if they were palm trees, grouped into pairs with the exception of those forming the two pavilions. Water flows in four channels, fed by the fountains in the Sala de los Abencerrajes and the Sala de las Dos Hermanas, and by those below the pavilions themselves. The Lion Fountain, which gives the entire palace its name, is one of the most beautiful exponents of Moorish-Granadan sculpture.

Each side of this patio leads into a different room. The **Sala de los Mocárabes** now communicates it with the Patio of the Myrtles, whilst the name of the **Sala de los Abencerrajes** recalls, it is said, the knights of this family whose throats were slit here during the period of internecine strife in the kingdom. Careful observation of the water in the fountain gives us a new perspective of the palace, the view reflected in it stretching from the magnificent mocarab dome covering this room to the Sala de las Dos Hermanas opposite. Next is the **Sala de los Reyes,** with its three alcoves. The parts now undecorated were formerly

Detail of the mural in the Comares Front, in the Mexuar Patio, showing the fine filigree of the stucco work.

The Sala de las Dos Hermanas («Room of the Two Sisters»).

A view of the Moorish Baths.

hung with curtains and carpets. The ceilings are decorated with 14th-century paintings on leather, representing the ten Nasrite kings and romantic and courtly scenes. Finally, we come to the **Sala de las Dos Hermanas** («Room of the Two Sisters»), whose name alludes to the two great slabs of marble in the floor near the central fountain. The upper dependencies were probably reserved for the women, who could attend parties and other social events without being seen, hidden behind ornamental wooden screens. This room opens up the Sala de los Ajimeces, with its salient belvederes, and culminates with the **Mirador de Daraxa,** one of the most romantic spots in the entire Alhambra. This belvedere, which conserves the only original stained-glass in the entire site, overlooks the beautiful **Garden of Daraxa,** behind which were built the **Rooms of Carlos V.** Washington Irving, author of the famous «Tales of the Alhambra» (1829) , once stayed in one of these rooms. Irving is much-loved in Granada, as he was one of the principal promoters of the

conservation of the Nasrite Palaces, which he found in a state of abandonment. In this section, we also find the **Moorish Baths,** dating to the reign of Yusuf I. The baths are arranged at different levels, each containing water at a different temperature. The main room has an upper gallery, reserved for the musicians. The Garden of Daraxa leads to the **Jardines del Partal,** which were installed after the Moorish period. Nevertheless, the Torre de las Damas («Tower of the Ladies»), the Oratory, or Torre del Mihrab and the so-called El Partal Houses were all built by the Muslims. In one of these houses are the remains of some interesting Moorish mural paintings The gardens form terraces stretching up to the **Church of Santa María de la Alhambra,** built in the 17th century on the site of the former mosque of the Medina of the Alhambra.
From here we can visit the Palace of Carlos V or continue on our way to the Generalife, adjoining the walls. The walls are made up of a double system of totally independent sentry walks, one over the curtain of the wall and the other at the lower part of the same. There is a tower every 150 metres approximately, the size and rich decoration of some of them making them resemble more small palaces. Their names, such as the Torre de la Cautiva («of

El Partal Gardens.

Palace of Carlos V and Church of Santa María de la Alhambra.

the Captive») or that of Las Tres Infantas («of the Three Princesses»), often evoke legends referring to the history of the palace. The emperor commissioned Pedro de Machuca with the construction of the **Palace of Carlos V** (3) in 1526. This work was left unfinished, however, and roofless, until it was completed in the present century. This is the most Italianate of mid-16th-century Spanish architecture, its style far from the preciosity of the Plateresque canon dominant at the time. Its grave, well-proportioned structure make it one of the most beautiful palaces in Spain, however, featuring a large circular courtyard measuring 30 metres in diameter, with two floors colonnaded with Doric columns on the lower floor and Ionic on the upper. Its excellent acoustics make this palace the ideal setting for the Granada International Music and Dance Festival. Inside, it houses the **Alhambra Museum,** containing a fine collection of pieces referring to Islamic culture in Spain, and the **Fine Art Museum,** whose collections include invaluable paintings and

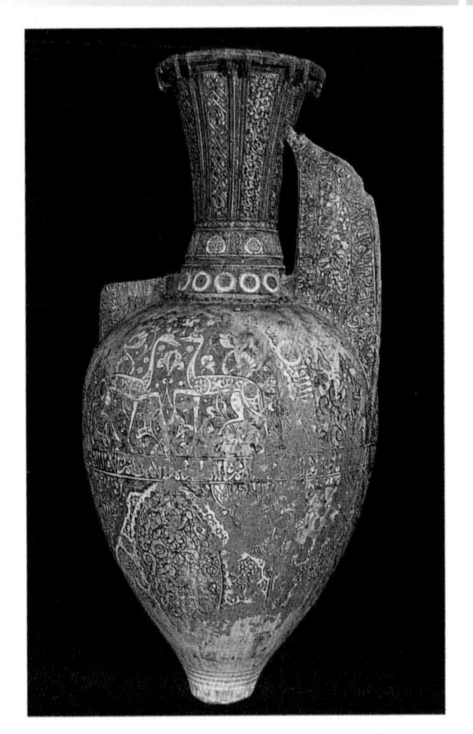

Jarrón de las Gacelas («Jar of the Gazelles») in the Alhambra Museum. Blue and gilt, this 14th-century work is considered a masterpiece of Spanish medieval ceramic art.

Triptych of El Gran Capitán, in the Fine Arts Museum. This is a work in Limoges enamel, dated around 1500, and attributed to the Pericaud brothers.

Patio de la Acequia in the Generalife.

sculptures dating from the 15th century to the present, mostly from the Granadan School.

A second route through the Alhambra Gardens towards the Generalife takes us through the area known as the Zona de Secano, an archaeological site currently under study. Opposite is the former **Convent of San Francisco,** now a Parador Nacional de Turismo, one of a chain of fine state-run hotels. The structure of this building reveals its original Moorish construction. Further on, on the hill known as the Cerro del Sol, stands the **Generalife (4),** once the summer palace of the Nasrite rulers. This building is organised around the delightful Patio de la Acequia, a courtyard of exuberant vegetation through the centre of which runs a long channel («acequia»), fed by water flowing from many fountain jets. Due to the many alterations carried out by the Catholic Monarchs, the physiognomy of the building is now much changed, but still conserves intact its truly spectacular beauty. The vegetable gardens which formerly surrounded the Generalife have long since

been transformed into lovely gardens, the incomparable setting of the Granada International Festival of Music and Dance.
We can now terminate this first itinerary by returning to the city centre by the south side of the Alhambra. This will allow us to visit a fine park, the **Carmen de los Mártires (5),** even though it is not a typical example of the Granadan *carmen.* The word comes from the Arabic *Karm,* vegetable garden, which came to signify a house and garden. The Carmen de los Mártires is made up of «romantic gardens» landscaped in the 19th century. Its position atop the hill commands panoramic views over the city. Finally, in Calle Antequeruela Alta, we come to the **Manuel de Falla House-Museum (6).** The great composer lived and wrote most of his oeuvre here. Born in Cádiz, he made Granada his residence for many years, from 1921 to 1939, when he left for America on an artistic engagement. Just a few years later, he died in Argentina. The house is conserved just as he left it, with all his personal effects in their place, making it an excellent exponent of the typical Granadan house of the period. Nearby is the **Manuel de Falla Auditorium,** which houses archives devoted to the composer, as well as his library and other important documents, such as scores and letters.

Manuel de Falla House-Museum: the composer's study.

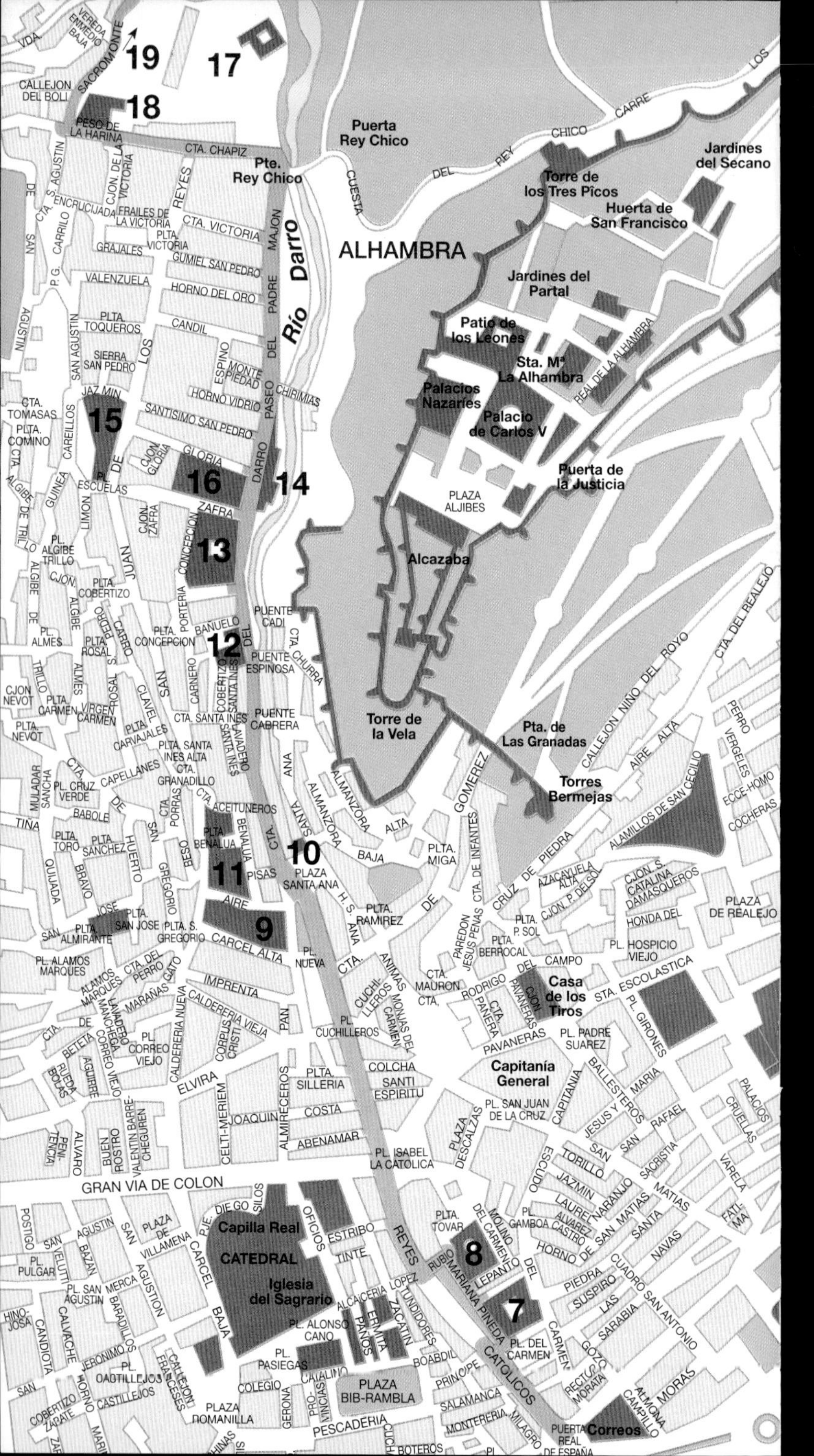

VDA.
VEREDA ENMEDIO BAJA
SACROMONTE
19
17
CALLEJON DEL BOLI
18
PESO DE LA HARINA
CTA. CHAPIZ
Puerta Rey Chico
Pte. Rey Chico
CUESTA DEL REY CHICO
CARRE LOS
Jardines del Secano
Torre de los Tres Picos
Huerta de San Francisco
ALHAMBRA
Río Darro
CJON. DE LA VICTORIA
REYES
S. AGUSTIN
CTA. CARRILO
ENCRUCIJADA
FRAILES DE LA VICTORIA
CTA. VICTORIA
PLTA. VICTORIA
GRAJALES
GUMIEL SAN PEDRO
VALENZUELA
HORNO DEL ORO
CANDIL
PLTA. TOQUEROS
SIERRA SAN PEDRO
SAN AGUSTIN
LOS
ESPINO
MONTE PIEDAD
PASEO DEL PADRE MAJON
CHIRIMIAS
HORNO VIDRIO
SANTISIMO SAN PEDRO
JAZ MIN
CTA. TOMASAS
PLTA. COMINO
CAREILLOS
15
DE
CJON. GLORIA
GLORIA
16
DARRO
14
Jardines del Partal
Patio de los Leones
Sta. Mª La Alhambra
REAL DE LA ALHAMBRA
Palacios Nazaríes
Palacio de Carlos V
Puerta de la Justicia
PLAZA ALJIBES
Alcazaba
CTA. ALGIBE DE TRILLO
GUINEA
PL. ESCUELAS
LIMON
CJON. ZAFRA
ZAFRA
CONCEPCION
13
PL. ALGIBE TRILLO
JUAN
CJON. ALGIBE
PLTA. COBERTIZO
PORTERIA
PUENTE CADI
CTA. CHURRA
PL. ALMES
PLTA. ROSAL
S. PEDRO
CARRO
PLTA. CONCEPCION
BAÑUELO
12
DEL
PUENTE ESPINOSA
CJON NEVOT
TRILLO
ALMES
ROSAL
CLAVEL
SAN
CARNERO
COBERTIZO SANTA INES
PLTA. CARMEN
VIRGEN CARMEN
PLTA. NEVOT
CTA. SANTA INES
PUENTE CABRERA
PLTA. CARVAJALES
PLTA. SANTA INES ALTA
LAVADERO SANTA INES
Torre de la Vela
Pta. de Las Granadas
CTA. DEL REALEJO
CALLEJON NIÑO DEL ROYO
PERRO
VERGELES
MULADAR SANCHA
CTA.
PL. CRUZ VERDE
CAPELLANES
CTA. GRANADILLO
ANA
SANTA
ALMANZORA
ALMANZORA ALTA
GOMEREZ
AIRE ALTA
Torres Bermejas
ECCE-HOMO
COCHERAS
TIÑA
BABOLE
DE
CTA. PORRAS
ACEITUNEROS
PLTA. BENALUA
BENALUA
CTA.
ALTA
ALAMILLOS DE SAN CECILIO
PLTA. TORO
PLTA. SANCHEZ
HUERTO
SAN
GREGORIO
BESO
10
PLAZA SANTA ANA
BAJA
PLTA. MIGA
CTA. DE INFANTES
QUIJADA
BRAVO
11
PISAS
AIRE
H. S. ANA
CRUZ DE PIEDRA
AZACAYUELA ALTA
CJON. P. DEL SOL
CJON. S. CATALINA
DAMASQUEROS
PLAZA DE REALEJO
JOSE
PLTA. SAN JOSE
PLTA. S. GREGORIO
9
CARCEL ALTA
PLTA. RAMIREZ
DE
PAREDON JESUS PEÑAS
PLTA. P. SOL
PLTA. BERROCAL
HONDA DEL
SAN
PL. ALMIRANTE
PL. NUEVA
CTA.
PL. HOSPICIO VIEJO
PL. ALAMOS MARQUES
CTA. DEL PERRO
ALAMOS MARQUES
GATO
IMPRENTA
ANIMAS
CUCHILLEROS
MONJAS DEL CARMEN
CTA. MAURON
CTA.
RODRIGO DEL CAMPO
CJON. PAVANERAS
Casa de los Tiros
STA. ESCOLASTICA
PL. GIRONES
MARAÑAS
LAVADERO
MANCHEGA
CALDERERIA NUEVA
CALDERERIA VIEJA
CTA. PANERA
CTA.
DE
BETETA
CORREO VIEJO
PL. CORREO VIEJO
CORPUS CRISTI
PAN
PL. CUCHILLEROS
PAVANERAS
PL. PADRE SUAREZ
RUEDA BOLAS
AGUIRRE
ELVIRA
PLTA. SILLERIA
COLCHA
SANTI ESPIRITU
Capitanía General
BALLESTEROS
MARIA
PALACIOS
CRUELLAS
CELTI-MERIEM
JOAQUIN
ALMIRECEROS
COSTA
PL. SAN JUAN DE LA CRUZ
CAPITANIA
JESUS Y
SAN
RAFAEL
PENI-TENCIA
ALVARO
BUEN ROSTRO
VALENTIN BARRE-CHEGUREN
ABENAMAR
PLAZA DESCALZAS
SAN
TORILLO
SACRISTIA
VARELA
PL. ISABEL LA CATOLICA
ESCUDO
JAZMIN
GRAN VIA DE COLON
MATIAS
LAUREL
ALVAREZ
NARANJO
PJE. DIE GO SILOS
OFICIOS
PLTA. TOVAR
DEL CARMEN
MOLINO
PL. GAMBOA
CASTRO
DE SAN MATIAS
FATIMA
POSTIGO
SAN AGUSTIN
SAN
PLAZA DE VILLAMENA
Capilla Real
ESTRIBO
REYES
8
HORNO
SANTA
SAN
VELUTTI
BAZAN
CARCEL
CATEDRAL
TINTE
RUBIO
LEPANTO
DEL
NAVAS
PL. PULGAR
AGUSTIN
CUADRO SAN ANTONIO
PL. SAN AGUSTIN
MERCA
BARADILLOS
Iglesia del Sagrario
LOPEZ
MARIANA PINEDA
PIEDRA
SUSPIRO
LAS
HINO-JOSA
CANDIOTA
CALVACHE
BAJA
ALCACERIA
ZACATIN
ERMITA
TUNDIDORES
7
CARMEN
SARABIA
PL. ALONSO CANO
PAÑOS
PL. DEL CARMEN
JERONIMO
PL. OAOTILLEJOS
CALLEJON FRANCESES
PL. PASIEGAS
CATALINO
BOABDIL
PRINCIPE
CATOLICOS
GOZO
RECTOR MORATA
ALMONA CAMPILLO
MORAS
SAN
COBERTIZO ZAPATE
HORNO
CASTILLEJOS
COLEGIO
GERONA
PRO-VINCIAS
PLAZA BIB-RAMBLA
SALAMANCA
PLAZA ROMANILLA
PESCADERIA
MONTERERIA
MILAGRO
PUERTA REAL DE ESPAÑA
Correos
BOTEROS

Town Hall.

II. FROM PUERTA REAL TO THE SACROMONTE

7. Town Hall
8. Corral del Carbón
9. Royal Chancellory
10. Church of Santa Ana
11. Casa de los Pisa
12. El Bañuelo
13. Convent of Santa Catalina de Zafra
14. Church of San Pedro y San Pablo
15. Church of San Juan de los Reyes
16. Casa de Castril (Archaeological Museum)
17. Palace of Los Córdoba
18. Casa del Chapiz (School of Arabic Studies)
19. Camino and Abbey of El Sacromonte.

This route takes in one of the most interesting itineraries around the city, showing us remains from all periods of history, but particularly Moorish and Renaissance works. As we follow the route, we shall ascend the River Darro, whose bed lies beneath the esplanade forming **Puerta Real**. Nevertheless, the river has run hidden to Plaza de Santa Ana since the mid-19th century, when this stretch was covered over. Until then, Calle de los Reyes Católicos had a similar aspect to Carrera

Patio of the Corral del Carbón.

del Darro, crossed by various bridges. Puerta Real is now the centre of the modern city, most of the busy shopping and business streets meeting here. Its name («Royal Gate») is due to the gate built here on occasion of the visit to the city of Philip IV in 1624.

In Plaza del Carmen stands the first monument of interest on this route: the **Town Hall (7),** which occupies the site of the former Convent of Carmelitas Calzadas, of which only the arcaded courtyard remains. Taking Calle Mariana de Pineda, we come to the **Corral del Carbón (8),** an interesting early-14th-century Moorish building, unique of its kind in Spain and conserved completely intact to our times. It was formerly the *Alhóndiga,* that is, inn and goods warehouse for merchants coming to the city. This type of establishment consisted of a small vestibule, used as a salon, and a patio for the stables, its galleries leading to the main dependencies, their structure preserved practically intact. The main front features great

decorative richness, particularly interesting in view of the fact that most Moorish buildings in Granada are characterised by external austerity. After the Christian conquest, the building fulfilled various uses, from the coal depot which gave it its present name, to *corral de comedias* (popular theatre) and residential building. It now contains craft shops and cultural information centres. Taking, Calle de los Reyes Católicos, one of the busiest thoroughfares in Granada, we come to Plaza de Isabel la Católica, presided over by a monument showing Columbus showing the queen his maps and plans. This sculpture, in stone and bronze, is by Mariano Benlliure in 1892. Further along, in Plaza Nueva, we come to the **Royal Chancellory (9),** one of the most outstanding palaces in Granada. It began to be built in 1530 and is organised around a central courtyard of two sections whose design is attributed to Diego de Siloé. A porch in this patio leads to a splendid staircase, the finest element in the entire palace due to its rich decoration and fine lighting. This was the chancellory and also housed a prison, installed at the rear of the building. The palace now serves as the seat of the Autonomous Community of Andalusia's High Court.
The square adjoining Plaza Nueva takes its name from the **Church of Santa Ana (10),** one of the loveliest in Granada

Plaza Nueva and the Church of Santa Ana. In the background, the Torre de la Vela.

El Bañuelo.

thanks to its slender, brick tower, adorned with *azulejos* (glazed tiles). This was designed by Diego de Siloé in around 1537 on the site of a small mosque founded by King Badis in the 11th century. The church contains important art works dating to the 16th and 17th centuries, including a sculpture of *La Dolorosa* by José de Mora.

In nearby Calle Convalescencia is the palace known as the **Casa de los Pisa (11),** now owned by the Order of Hospitallers. The building houses a museum devoted to Saint John of God, who died here in 1550.

Carrera del Darro is one of the finest thoroughfares in Granada. During Moorish times, a wall was built here, parallel to the river, with bridges connecting the Alhambra with the Albaicín district of the city. In the early-16th century, this wall was demolished to make way for the construction along the new street of churches and aristocratic houses. Nevertheless, a number of Moorish buildings still survive here, including the so-called **Bañuelo (12).** These were public baths, amongst the oldest (they were built in the 11th century) and best-conserved in Spain. Their structure is typical of *hammams,* or Moorish baths: a vestibule leads to the different rooms, which have cold, warm or hot water. The room with cold water is the largest, whilst the hot water room is characterised by its thicker walls and lower vaults to retain the steam. Underground is the heater with an oven and channels leading to a great tank of boiler water. The main room of El Bañuelo is regular in shape, porticoed with horseshoe arches adorned by a variety of Roman, Visigoth and Caliphal capitals. The ceiling is full of star-shaped skylights which were originally covered with coloured alabaster, through which entered a tinted light, filtered through the billowing steam, conferring on the baths a special atmosphere, heightened even more by the aroma of the perfume holders. Opposite the baths are the ruins of the **Puente del Cadí,** a bridge built during the reign of King Badis,

Church of San Pedro y San Pablo, in Carrera del Darro.

Casa del Castril, seat of the Archaeological Museum.

formerly the main communication between the Alhambra and the Albaicín.

After admiring the Puente del Cadí, we come to various churches: the **Convent of Santa Catalina de Zafra (13),** the **Church of San Pedro y San Pablo (14)** and, further on, the **Convent of San Bernardo,** all of which began to be built in the 16th century. In the interior of the Convent of Santa Catalina de Zafra is a Moorish house, its courtyard, with cistern and galleries, reminiscent of the Mexuar in the Alhambra. Another outstanding religious building in this area is the **Church of San Juan de los Reyes (15),** in the street of the same name. This was the converts' mosque, frequented by Christians who had given up their faith, for which reason, no doubt, it was the first parish church in Granada to be blessed by the Catholic Monarchs. Of the original late-13th century construction it retains the minaret, now converted into a belltower. This is Almohade in style, with rising ramps in the interior. The experts agree in qualifying the tower as the sister of the famed Giralda in Seville.

Opposite the Church of San Pedro y San Pablo is the Casa de

Castril (16), a fine example of the noble houses of its time. Its elaborately-ornamented façade is remarkable: over the lintel is the escutcheon the Catholic Monarchs granted to Hernando de Zafra, their secretary, whose heirs owned this house. It now houses the **Granada Archaeological and Ethnological Museum.** This is divided into seven rooms devoted to the different civilisations which have left their mark on Granada from the city's prehistoric origins to the Christian conquest.
At the end of Carrera del Darro stretches Paseo del Padre Majón, popularly known as **Paseo de los Tristes** («Promenade of the Sad Ones») as this was where funeral corteges used to pass. Paseo de los Tristes commands fine views over the Alhambra and the *cármenes* on the other side of the river: that of Chirimías, adjoining the bridge of the same name, and that of Los Chapiteles, former residence of El Gran Capitán, on the other side of the Alijibillo bridge. This bridge leads to two paths, El Camino del Avellano, rising to the top of the mountain, and the Camino del Rey Chico, leading to the Alhambra

Palace of los Córdoba.

Casa del Chapiz.

and of particular interest for the different views it offers of the Nasrite Palaces and the surrounding walls.
Cuesta del Chapiz begins at the end of Paseo de los Tristes. At number 4, surrounded by beautiful gardens opposite the Alhambra, is the **Palacio de los Córdoba (17).** This palace was completely rebuilt after it was transferred here from Gran Vía. It is Renaissance in style, arranged around a patio with Gothic elements and Mudéjar coffering. It was inaugurated in 1983 as the seat of the Historic Archives of Granada, open to scholars only.
Higher up, next to the tiny Plaza del Peso de la Harina, is the Granada School of Arabic Studies, installed in the **Casa del Chapiz (18).** The site is formed by two «Morisco» with later Christian additions. A visit to this palace is of particular interest due to its harmonious mixture of elements from different styles and cultures, making it a fine exponent of the civil architecture born after the Christian conquest.

Plaza del Peso de la Harina marks the beginning of the **Camino del Sacromonte (19),** leading to the *barrio,* quarter, of the same name, famed for its Gypsy cave houses. The path, dotted by a *via crucis,* culminates at the Hermitage of the Santo Sepulcro, founded in the 17th century, continuing along the so-called seven crests or *revueltas,* ending at the Collegiate Church of San Cecilio, or **Abbey of El Sacromonte (19).** This site contains the Abbey, the seminary and the College. It was founded in the early-17th century as a result of the discovery in the nearby **Santas Cuevas** («Holy Caves») of the relics of various martyrs, among them Saint Cecilio, first bishop of Granada and patron saint of the city. Though the discovery later turned out to be false, religious processions still take place to the Santas Cuevas, particularly on the saint's day, 1 February. The Abbey contains many fine works of art: paintings, sculptures, codices, incunabula and Arabic manuscripts, this last collection housed in a monographic museum. Another attraction of a visit to El Sacromonte are the magnificent views over the city, the plains and the Sierra Nevada. After this last stop on our itinerary, we return to Cuesta del Chapiz, the starting-point of the next, which will take us into the Albaicín.

Abbey of El Sacromonte.

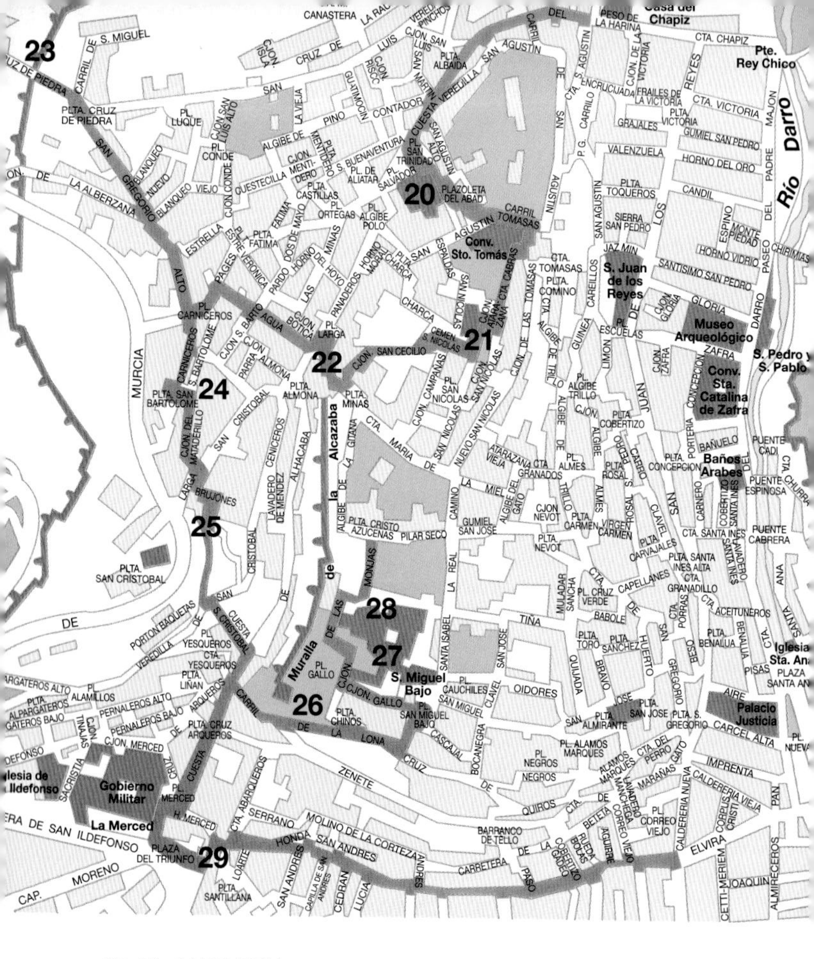

III. EL ALBAICIN

20. Church of El Salvador
21. Belvedere and Church of San Nicolás
22. Puerta Nueva or Arco de las Pesas
23. Puerta de Fajalauza
24. Church of San Bartolomé
25. Belvedere and Church of San Cristóbal
26. Puerta Monaita
27. Convent of Santa Isabel la Real
28. Palace of Dar Al Horra
29. Puerta de Elvira.

We enter the Albaicín, linking up with the previous itinerary, from Cuesta del Chapiz, a road leading into Plaza del Salvador. The origins of the Albaicín district go back to the birth of the city itself, for this hill was the site of the first Iberian and Roman settlements. There are various theories as to the origin of the name of this district. Some affirm that it derives from the Arabic word *Al Bayyasin,* meaning «those from Baeza», as the Moors from that city in Jaen province settled here after it had fallen to the armies of Ferdinand the Holy. Others, however, claim that the name comes from *albayyazín,* making this the «falconers' quarter», whilst the 14th-century, Granadan historian Al Jathib defined the meaning of the word Albaicín most appropriately as «the district on a crest».

The layout of the district is fundamentally Moorish. The ruins remain of a double wall which formerly encircled it, the internal walls built in the 11th century by the Ziri dynasty. Inside these walls was the Alcazaba Cadima, their palace, now lost. The constant growth of the city later obliged the construction of a second encircling wall and, according to records dating to the surrender of Granada, the Albaicín had a population of 60,000 souls and as many as 26 mosques, twelve of them converted into churches and the rest demolished. After the Christian reconquest, the district lost its Muslim inhabitants, replaced by Christians who built fine palaces here. The population of the Albaicín gradually fell, its history to the present day full of ups and downs, periods of wealth alternating with others of abandonment.

Overall view of the Albaicín from the Alhambra.

The Alhambra, seen from the Balcón de San Nicolás.

Today, the Albaicín is a treasury of magnificent Moorish and Christian monuments, made even more attractive by its unusual geographical features, commanding fine views over the district itself, the city and the Alhambra. Walking around this labyrinth of narrow streets, the visitor feels drawn back into the history of Granada, for time does not appear to have passed for many nooks and corners here. We notice that the lack of parks and gardens is made up for by the ***cármenes***, house-gardens, some of them with of them boasting the most exuberant vegetation. We also come across many ***aljibes***, fountains, of different types, which formerly supplied the quarter with water, and which are now mostly in disuse.

Our first stop is in **Plaza del Salvador.** At one end of this square is a Morisco house, known as the Casa de Yanguas. This has Nasrite, Gothic and Renaissance decoration, and is another exponent of Granadan civil architecture after the reconquest. At one corner is a fountain known as the Aljibe del

Polo, whilst the square is dominated by the **Church of El Salvador (20).** This was built in the 16th century on the site of the main mosque of the Albaicín, of which part of the *sahn,* or patio of ablutions, remains. The church was destroyed by fire in 1936, only the walls and arches of the great nave surviving, and was restored in 1950. Of the original work, an outstanding element is the fine stone portal, designed by Diego de Siloé. From Plaza del Salvador we go on to Plaza del Abad, which features the Aljibe de Bib-al-Bunud. Taking Calleja de las Tomasas into Cuesta de las Cabras we skirt around the Convent of Santo Tomás de Villanueva, known as the Convent of Las Tomasas. The architecture of this monument blends perfectly into the overall panorama of the Albaicín. Cuesta de las Cabras leads to the **Mirador and Church of San Nicolás (21),** one of the finest belvederes in the entire city and an excellent point from which to admire both city, the Alhambra and, in the background, the Sierra Nevada. The church, which stands on the site of a former mosque, was also burnt down during the Spanish Civil War, and was later rebuilt.

Church of San Cristóbal.

Main street in San Bartolomé, and church belltower.

We now take Callejón de San Cecilio, with the **Puerta de Hizna-Román,** now converted into the Chapel of San Cecilio. This was the gate to the former Alcazaba Cadima until the 11th century, when the Ziries restored the old walls of the Alcazaba and this gate was closed and replaced by , **Puerta Nueva or the Arch of las Pesas (22)** at the end of the little street. Thanks to the strength of the mortar used in its construction, Puerta Nueva is conserved practically intact. It has a zigzag structure and a large turret. Through it runs Plaza Large which, though a small square, is very busy and bustling with activity, as it is the main central thoroughfare in the Albaicín district. From here branch out such important streets as Calle del Agua, where once stood some Moorish baths which, according to the chronicles, were the largest in Granada.

Calle del Agua terminates in Calle de Pagés. From here we can take Calle de San Gregorio Alto to reach the Placeta de la Cruz de Piedra, adjoining which stands the **Puerta de Fajalauza (23),** a gate with barrel vault and minaret which formerly marked the beginning of the road to Guadix. From the square, we take Carril de San Miguel, which leads to the Hermitage of San Miguel, built in a turret which formed part of the old city walls.
Back in Calle Pagés, we enter the nearby Plaza de San Bartolomé, which contains the **Church of San Bartolomé (24).** This church stands on the site of the old Burriana mosque, of which the *aljibe* is conserved. Its most outstanding feature, however, is its fine Mudéjar tower, one of the most lovely in Granada. Callejón del Matadero and then Brujones now lead us to the **Mirador and Church of San Cristóbal (25),** adjoining the Murcia road. This is the highest point in the Albaicín district, at an altitude of 773 metres, and commands views over practically the entire city: the popular «barrichuelo» Albaicín district at the foot of the belvedere and, opposite, the remains of the old city walls, behind which we can make out

Puerta Monaita.

Palace of Dar Al Horra.

the Palace of Dar al Horra and the Convent of Santa Isabel la Real. Due to the ups and downs of its history, the Church of San Cristóbal is much altered now from its original form. Built on the site of the Axarea mosque, it once boasted the tallest tower in the city.
We continue our route at the foot of this mirador, where typical narrow zigzagging streets cut into the mountain –a total of 120 steps– take us to Cuesta de Alhabaca. One of the streets crossing this «crest» leads to the **Puerta Monaita (26),** once the entrance to the Alcazaba Cadima. Next, we take Carril de la Lona, which commands fine views over the western part of the city, to Plaza de San Miguel Bajo. Presiding over this square is the Church of San Miguel, like so many Granadan churches originally a mosque.
The Convent of **Santa Isabel la Real (27)** and the **Palace of Dar al Horra (28)** stand on site of the old Ziri Alcazaba. The convent has a fine Elizabethan portal, attributed to Enrique Egas, and the

interior is beautifully decorated in the Plateresque style. The Palace of Dar al Horra is a 15th-century construction which served as the residence of the Sultana Aixa, mother of Boabdil, who moved here after being repudiated by her husband, Muley Hacen, who had fallen in love with the beautiful Zoraya, none other than Isabel de Solís, the captive of Martos.
We now retrace our steps to Cuesta de Alhabaca, from where the next stop is the monumental **Puerta de Elvira (29),** once the city's principal gate. The remains which survive –a giant exterior Moorish arch– date to the 11th century, though its existence is recorded as far back as the 9th. Visitors are now recommended to return to the city centre via **Calle de Elvira,** the principal thoroughfare in Moorish Granada, separating the Albaicín district from the administrative and commercial centre, along with the main mosque, on the site of which the Cathedral now stands.

Plateresque portal of the Convent of Santa Isabel la Real.

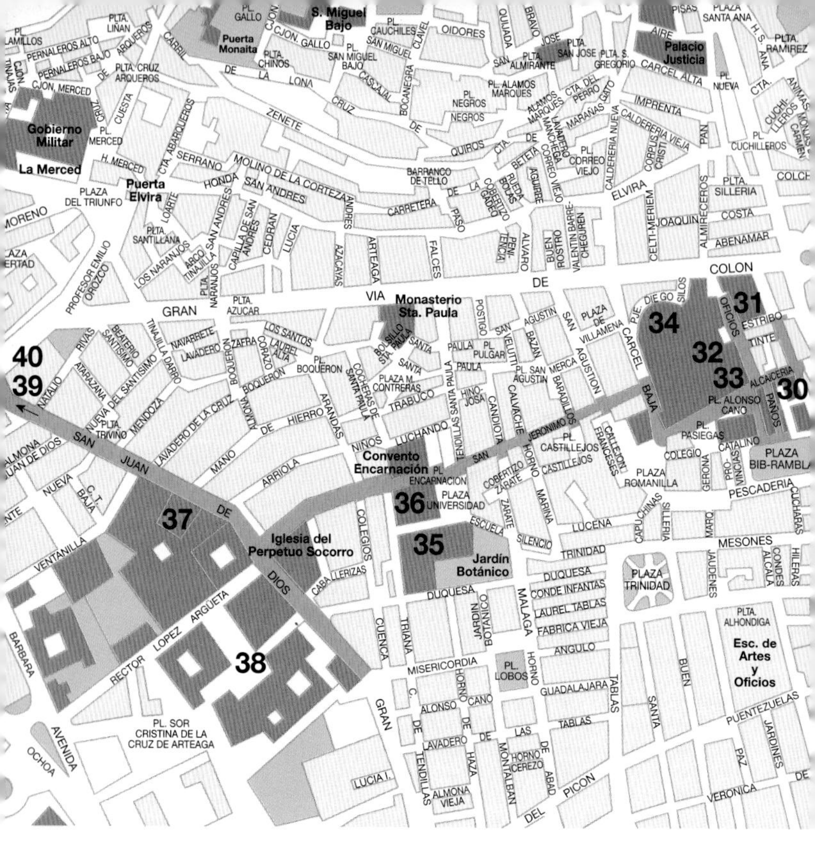

IV. FROM ZACATIN TO THE CARTHUSIAN MONASTERY

30. Alcaicería
31. La Madraza
32. Chapel Royal
33. Church of El Sagrario
34. Cathedral
35. University
36. Church of Los Santos Justo y Pastor
37. Hospital and Church of San Juan de Dios
38. Monastery of San Jerónimo
39. Royal Hospital
40. The Cartuja (Carthusian Monastery).

This itinerary takes in two broad areas. The first, the Cathedral site and immediate vicinity, includes a zone which formed the administrative and commercial centre of Granada during the Nasrite era, as well as being the site of the main mosque. The

second zone, from the University to the Cartuja, or Carthusian Monastery, dates in its entirety to the period after the Christian reconquest, when urban expansion brought with it the demolishment of part of the old city walls so that the surrounding land could be built upon.
We include in this route the popular **Calle del Zacatín,** Granada's main thoroughfare up to the late-19th century, when the parallel Calle de los Catholic Monarchs was opened up. El Zacatín (an Arabic word meaning «old clothes dealers») has always been a centre for trade and commerce, and still is. Here, testifying the importance of the area during Muslim times, were Moorish baths, the *alhóndiga,* or exchange, and the House of Justice. Halfway along the street is the **Alcaicería (30),** or Moorish silk market, the city's main zoco where the most sumptuous goods were bought and sold. In its time, the Alcaicería was much larger and functioned as an independent «village». The accesses to it were closed at night and it had its own mosque and customs house. A terrible fire in 1843 destroyed it completely, though it was rebuilt exactly as before.
Various streets lead from the Alcaicería or the Zacatín itself into **Plaza de Bib-Rambla.** This square, site of the fish and

A view of the Alcaicería.

Plaza de Bib-Rambla.

meat markets, was much smaller during Moorish times, but was extended after the Christian reconquest to fulfil the role of the city's main square and the principal site of fiestas and celebrations. In the centre is the original Fountain of Los Gigantones, dedicated to Neptune. This was made from Elvira stone in the 17th century, though not installed in this square until 1940. The leafy lime trees which populate the square, the rich colour and scent of its flower stalls and the constant murmuring of the fountain give this square, which has never relinquished its status as an important centre of the city, a particular charm. On one side stands the austere building of the **Episcopal Palace.**

We now take Calle Oficios leaving to the left the Episcopal Palace, the Church of El Sagrario, the Cathedral, the Chapel Royal and the Exchange which, along with the adjoining 16th-century building housing the Curia or Old University, occupies the site of the old main mosque. On the right, opposite the

Chapel Royal, is the Baroque façade of the building which houses **La Madraza (31),** the Moorish university founded by Yusuf I in 1349 and which became the principal centre of culture in Islamic Spain. Its illustrious students include such great sages as Ibn al-Jatib, politician, poet and city historian, or the great poet Ibn Zamrak, whose verses are reproduced in various rooms of the Alhambra. After the Reconquest, the Catholic Monarchs donated it for use as a Chapterhouse. Successive alterations, however, completely changed the original appearance and organisation of the building. Conserved, though much-restored, from the original building is the oratory opposite the main entrance, at the rear of the patio in accordance with the traditional arrangement of such constructions. It has a square ground plan with *mihrab,* and is richly adorned with stucco, stalactites and inscriptions, giving the visitor a glimpse of the importance this building once enjoyed.

Oratory of La Madraza.

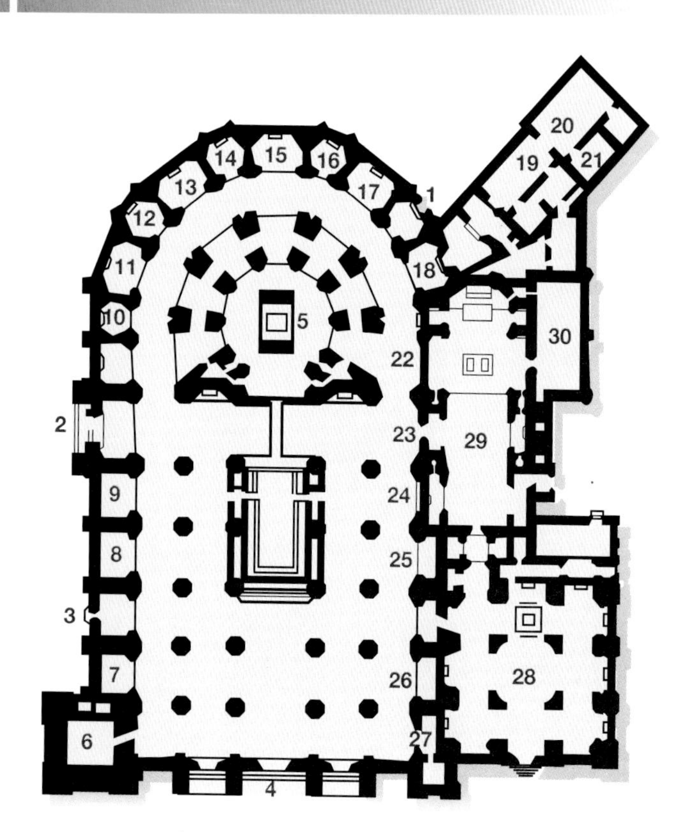

1. Door of El Ecce Homo.
2. Door of El Perdón.
3. Door of San Jerónimo.
4. Main front.
5. High Chapel.
6. Cathedral treasure.
7. Chapel of the Virgen del Pilar.
8. Chapel of the Virgen del Carmen.
9. Chapel of Nuestra Señora de las Angustias.
10. Chapel of Nuestra Señora de la Antigua.
11. Chapel of Santa Lucía.
12. Chapel of El Cristo de las Penas.
13. Chapel of Santa Teresa.
14. Chapel of San Blas.
15. Chapel of San Cecilio.
16. Chapel of San Sebastián.
17. Chapel of Santa Ana.
18. Portal of the sacristy.
19. Antesacristy.
20. Sacristy.
21. Chapterhouse.
22. Altarpiece of El Apóstol Santiago.
23. Portal of the Chapel Royal.
24. Altarpiece of Jesús Nazareno.
25. Chapel of la Trinidad.
26. Chapel of San Miguel.
27. Cathedral Museum.
28. Church of El Sagrario.
29. Chapel Royal.
30. Sacristy-Museum.

The **Chapel Royal (32)** is entered through the old Goods Exchange («Lonja de Mercaderes»), a fine rectangular building with semicircular arches supported by columns decorated by cords and capitals with Gothic leaves. The upper floor had Gothic balconies. The main front of the Chapel Royal was integrated into the Cathedral, and the outer doorway giving onto the square is a secondary entrance for the chapter to enter from their house nearby. This second door is Plateresque in style and is crowned by a small roof.
The Chapel Royal was ordered built by the Catholic Monarchs to house their burial places, and was duly founded to that end in 1504, though both died before it was finished and their mortal remains lay in the Convent of San Francisco de la Alhambra until they were transferred in 1521. The building was designed by Enrique Egas and is a fine exponent of the late-Gothic and Renaissance styles. The building has a Latin cross ground plan with four side chapels. The decoration features particularly the coats of arms and initials of the founders, emblems which appear on all the walls. The crossing is closed

Lonja de Mercaderes («Exchange») and portal of the Chapel Royal.

«Triptych of the Passion», by Dierik Bouts (Chapel Royal Museum).

by a magnificent monumental grille, wrought in 1520 by Bartolomé de Jaén. Behind it are the royal tombs, an exquisite, complex work in Carrara marble. The tombs of the Catholic Monarchs are by the Italian artist Domenico Fancelli in 1517, whilst those of Philip the Handsome and Juana the Mad are the work of Bartolomé Ordóñez and date to 1519 and 1520 respectively. Below, steps lead down to the crypt containing the coffins of the four monarchs and Prince Michael, grandson of the Catholic Monarchs. Presiding over the high altar is a fine Italianate altarpiece by Felipe Vigarny, completed between 1520 and 1522. Flanking it are the praying figures of the Catholic Monarchs, Ferdinand and Isabel, sculptures attributed to Diego de Siloé.
The Sacristy contains the **Chapel Royal Museum,** which features a collection of royal possessions such as King Ferdinand's sword and scabbard and Isabel's crown and sceptre, as well as her mirror, converted into a monstrance.

There is also a good collection of Flemish and Italian painting, featuring masterpieces by Van de Weyden, Hans Momling and Perugino amongst others.
Adjoining the Chapel Royal is the **Church of El Sagrario (33).** The main entrance is in Plaza de Alonso Cano, exactly on the site of the entrance to the mosque, which was converted into a church. Nevertheless, this building was allowed to fall into a ruinous state, and the present church was built in its stead in the 18th century.
The **Cathedral (34)** was built by express order of Queen Isabel. It was designed in Gothic style by Enrique Egas and work began on it in 1523, to be continued, transformed into Renaissance style, by Diego de Siloé after 1528. The result, considered one of the finest of Spanish Renaissance religious buildings, is a Renaissance church on a Gothic ground plan. It was finally completed in 1704, when the Cathedral was inaugurated. Various architects directed the works over this

The artistic grille and the royal tombs in the Chapel Royal.

long period of construction, including, amongst others, Alonso Cano, author of the main front (1667), outstanding in its simplicity and originality. One tower is unfinished and the other never began to be built. Other outstanding elements include the Puerta del Perdón and that of San Jerónimo, both by Diego de Siloé.

Once inside the Cathedral, the visitor is surprised by the dazzling luminosity of the building, an effect achieved by the studied play of light entering through the stained-glass windows and the white of the walls, this colour, along with gilt, dominating the colour scheme throughout. The Cathedral has a nave and four aisles, side chapels and dome, and reaches an extraordinary height. The **Capilla Mayor,** a masterpiece by Diego de Siloé, is a veritable architectural jewel. It occupies an almost circular area 22 metres in diameter, the crossing at its highest point reaching a height of 45 metres. The Capilla Mayor is also beautifully illuminated by its 16th-century Flemish stained-glass windows. The paintings in the upper storey, by Alonso Cano, depict scenes from the life of the Virgin, whilst the columns surrounding the chapel feature carvings of apostles and saints. Also admirable are the two colossal baroque organs, the work of Fernández y Dávila in 1745, and the collection of choir books. In the nave is a pantheon containing, amongst others, the tombs of Alonso Cano and Mariana Pineda.

Aerial view of the Cathedral.

Capilla Mayor of the Cathedral.

Of the various side chapels, the most interesting are those of Nuestra Señora de las Angustias, by José de Bada, and Nuestra Señora de la Antigua. In the latter there is a 15th-century statue of the Virgin which gives the chapel its name, formerly the patron saint of Granada, apparently brought here by the Catholic Monarchs after taking the city. The tower contains the Cathedral museum which, though small, nevertheless features important paintings and pieces, including, outstandingly, Alonso Cano's sculpture of the Immaculate.
After the visit to the Cathedral, we take Calle San Jerónimo to Plaza Universidad. The **University (35)** and the **Church of San Justo y Pastor (36)** originally formed part of a Jesuit convent until their expulsion in 1767. The church, built in the late-16th

Hospital and Church of San Juan de Dios.

century, presents austerely elegant classical forms with later Baroque elements of striking sumptuousness. The altarpiece over the high altar is a good illustration of this. The adjoining building, now the Law Faculty, housed the Literary University founded by Charles V in 1526. Of the original building only the Baroque portal and a room or two survive. At the rear is a Botanical Garden installed in the 19th century after a number of old buildings were demolished.

We now continue along Calle San Jerónimo to Gran Capitán, where we can admire various noble buildings: the San Bartolomé y Santiago High School, the palaces of Caicedo and Ansoti, now the Conservatory and the Notaries College respectively, and the former Church of San Felipe Neri, now that of El Perpetuo Socorro.

The **Hospital and Church of San Juan de Dios (37)** occupy the original site of the Monastery of San Jerónimo, a building altered to conform to Renaissance tastes. Nevertheless, the church dates to the 18th century and is a veritable exponent of the most exuberant Baroque style, particularly as regards the high altarpiece, in clearly Churrigueresque style, by Francisco Guerrero. A door in the high chapel leads into a little chamber where, amongst the profuse decoration, are kept relics of the saint, as well as his stick and the basket with which he begged for alms.

The **Monastery of San Jerónimo (38)** was founded in 1492 by the Catholic Monarchs in the town of Santa Fe, but it was later transferred to its present site here. It is a late-Gothic construction with clearly Renaissance elements. The work was directed by Jacobo Florentino, El Indaco, and, after his death in 1526, Diego de Siloé, who also built some of the portals in the cloisters. The cloister provides entrance to the church, the initial darkness having the effect of giving greater light to the magnificent, monumental altarpiece at the head of the building, a masterpiece of Spanish sculpture. This element has four

View of the cloister of the Monastery of San Jerónimo.

Campo del Triunfo and the Royal Hospital.

sections featuring the Doric, Ionic, Corinthian and composite orders successively. Flanking the altarpiece are the praying figures of the Gran Capitán and his wife, to whom King Charles V gave this chapel as a family burial-place. Gonzalo Fernández de Córdoba, the Gran Capitán, lies under a burial stone at the foot of the staircase. Before leaving the church, we should pause to admire the fine choirstalls by Diego de Siloé in 1544. Calle Gran Capitán and then Calle San Juan de Dios lead into the **Campo de Triunfo.** This great irregular-shaped, sloping esplanade has witnessed many chapters in the history of Granada. There originally stood here, apparently, a Visigoth basilica, which was destroyed by the Almohades to make way for a cemetery. After the Christian conquest, churches and noble houses were built around it, including the former **Royal Hospital (39),** founded by the Catholic Monarchs in 1504 for the poor and pilgrims. It is now the seat of the Rectory and other University services. During the French invasion and later

it was a place of executions, and it was here that Mariana Pineda, a heroine of the fight for freedom, was put to death in 1831. After laying abandoned for many years, in around 1950 it was decided to install gardens here, as well as the monument to the Immaculate Conception or the Virgin of Triumph, which formerly stood by the Puerta de Elvira.
We complete this itinerary at the **Cartuja, or Carthusian Monastery (40).** This stands to the north of the city, and was founded in the 16th century. The austerity of the exterior and the monastery itself give way to the surprising Baroque exuberance of the church, particularly the Sacristy and *Sancta Sanctorum,* startling in their rich ornamentation with constant plays of forms, perspective and lights. The Sacristy, commenced in 1727 is the work of Luis de Arévalo and Luis Cabello, who took 37 years to complete it. It is presided over by a large sculpture of Saint Bruno. The Sancta Sanctorum is a prodigious work by Francisco Hurtado Izquierdo and features paintings by Palomino and sculptures by Risueño. In the centre is a large, sumptuous tabernacle made from marble of different colours and tones in which the sacrary is kept.

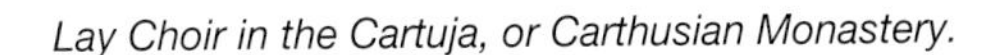

Lay Choir in the Cartuja, or Carthusian Monastery.

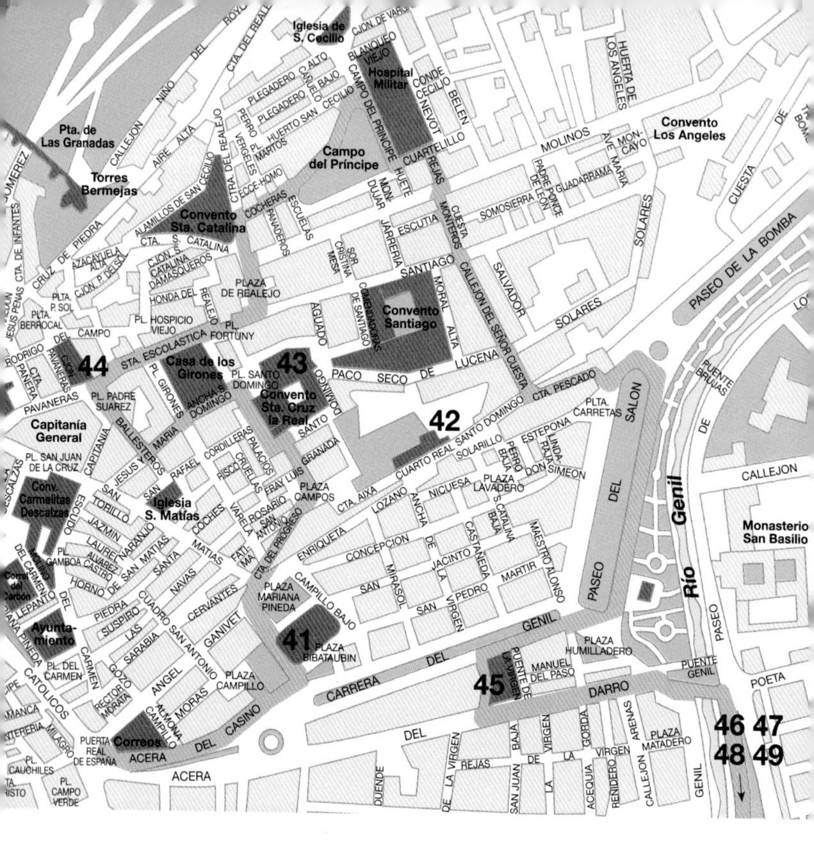

V. FROM PUERTA REAL TO THE CAMPO DEL PRINCIPE AND FROM THE RIVER GENIL TO THE SCIENCE PARK

41. Provincial Government building
42. Cuarto Real of Santo Domingo
43. Church of Santo Domingo
44. Casa de los Tiros
45. Basilica of Nuestra Señora de las Angustias
46. Hermitage of San Sebastián
47. Alcázar Genil
48. Federico García Lorca House-Museum
49. Science Park.

The zone featured in this route came into being after the Christian reconquest, occupying a large area of gardens and vegetable gardens outside the city walls, with the exception of the districts at the foot of the Torres Bermejas. This was the site of the old Jewish quarter, the home of the community formed outside the walls of old Roman *Iliberris* and whose name was *Garnata al Yahud.* Though none of its buildings survive, this is the only Jewish heritage the city can claim, despite the long period the community lived in Granada.

From Puerta Real, we take Acera del Casino to **Plaza de Campillo Bajo,** a square with a fine central fountain in neoclassical style, surrounded by hundred-year-old plane trees. During Moorish times, this was where the Puerta de Bibataubín, or Gate of Penitence, stood. This was a castle-turret over whose remains now stands the seat of the **Provincial Government (Diputación, 41).** This is an 18th-century building easily recognised by the Solomonic (barley-sugar) columns of its portal. Behind is **Plaza de Mariana Pineda,** featuring a monument to that local heroine and champion of freedom. In nearby **Calle de San Matías** is the church of the same name, a 16th-century Gothic-Mudéjar building, though later alteration has hidden its original appearance. It features fine Plateresque portals, and contains works by José Risueño and Bocanegra. **Calle Navas,** which crosses Calle de San Matías, is one of the most popular streets in the city, containing many tapas bars.

Fountain of La Acera del Casino. In the background, the provincial government building.

Cuarto Real de Santo Domingo.

Returning to Plaza de Mariana Pineda, we now take Cuesta del Progreso to Plaza de los Campos to visit the **Cuarto Real de Santo Domingo (42).** Half-hidden amongst gardens and later buildings, this is a Moorish construction dating back to the 13th century which is thought to have been used by the kings of Granada as a place of retreat during Ramadan. A single tower is conserved from the original Moorish palace, housing a square room leading off to alcoves and small balconies adorned with lattices. The decoration consists of stucco work, directly carved and painted, as well as *alicatados.* The ornamentation is particularly interesting as, since the dynasty's motto is not present in it, it can be dated to just before or during the reign of the first Nasrite king.
We now continue from Plaza de los Campos to Plaza de Santo Domingo, where we find the **Convent of Santa Cruz la Real** and the **Church of Santo Domingo (43),** both buildings commenced in the 16th century. The convent, founded by the

Catholic Monarchs in an action of thanksgiving for the conquest of Granada, is now but a shadow of what it used to be: one of the finest and most important of the period. The Church of Santo Domingo originally belonged to the convent. It began to be built in Gothic style, but the masonry and decoration are Renaissance. The church has a fine portal made up of a stone porch over which is a Plateresque window. The interior has a ground plan in the form of a Latin cross with side chapels whose vaults feature Gothic ribbing. The church also contains interesting carvings and paintings from different periods.
In nearby Calle Ancha de Santo Domingo is the **Casa de los Girones,** which has belonged to the Téllez Girón family since the 16th century. This house stands on the site of an old Moorish palace of which only a room decorated with carved stucco and polychrome *alicatado* (arrangements of glazed tiles) survives. The building was recently restored as the seat of the Granada International Festival of Music and Dance. In nearby **Plaza del Padre Suárez** stand a further two interesting noble houses. These are the house which gives the square its name, birth-place of that famous Granadan Jesuit, known as «Doctor Eximio», and now the seat of the Archives of the Royal

Coffering in the Gold Room of the Casa de los Tiros.

The Corral del Carbón according to a 19th-century engraving, the original of which is in the Casa de los Tiros.

Chancellory, and the **Casa de los Tiros (44)**, whose name («House of Shots») derives from the muskets which point out from its battlements of its turret. The fortified nature of the building is due to the fact that it once formed part of the old city walls. The building dates to the first half of the 16th century, the same period as the main room, or Cuadra Dorada, which has a fine ceiling of carved wood and contains busts in haut relief and inscriptions alluding to Spanish kings and heroes. The Casa de los Tiros now houses the Library and Newspaper Library on the subject themes concerning the city of Granada. Its exhibits include a magnificent collection of engravings by a variety of artists from different periods. Some of these go a long way back

in history, giving us a vision of the city at different times. Besides the permanent exhibition, temporary exhibitions are also organised here, devoted particularly to local arts and crafts.
We now take Santa Escolástica to **Plaza del Realejo,** which still conserves its original flavour. This was once the centre of the Jewish quarter, and was later occupied by Morisco ceramists and weavers. Next, Calle Cocheras leads to **Campo del Príncipe,** which was formerly occupied by vegetable and flower gardens. The stone Cross of Elvira with the image of El Cristo de los Favores was installed in 1640 and is the object of great popular veneration, particularly on Good Friday, when crowds of faithful come here to ask for the traditional three «favours». Adjoining the square is the **Military Hospital,** housed in a 16th-century palace, and the **Church of San Cecilio,** built over an earlier church where the Christians are thought to have worshipped under Moorish rule. The present building dates to around 1530, but is now in a poor state of repair after being damaged by fire. Behind the church is the old quarter of **La Antequeruela,** whose name alludes to the Moors of that city in Jaen province who settled here after its conquest by the Christian army in the year 1410.

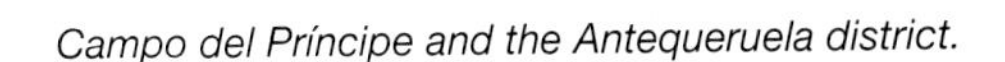

Campo del Príncipe and the Antequeruela district.

Congress Palace.

We now return to our itinerary along the **River Genil,** going along Paseo del Salón and Paseo de la Bomba. These promenades were opened up in the mid-18th century and were recently reformed, providing pleasant gardens much frequented by locals and visitors alike. At the end of Paseo del Salón, we take Carrera del Genil to visit the **Basilica of Nuestra Señora de las Angustias (45)** devoted to the patron saint of Granada. This was built in the 17th century and features graceful belltowers. In the portal is a statue of the Virgin holding the body of Christ, by Bernardo de Mora and his son José. Beside this is another simple portal giving entrance to the sacristy. The church contains a fine Churrigueresque *camarín* in which is kept an image of *Nuestra Señora de las Angustias,* the work of Duque Cornejo. We now cross to river to continue along Paseo del Violón. Opposite the impressive modern structure of the **Congress Palace,** past some pleasant gardens, is the **Hermitage of San Sebastián (46),** a former Moorish *morabito,* the only one of its

type conserved from the Nasrite period. On one of its façades is a plaque commemorating the surrender of the city here by Boabdil, last of the Nasrite kings, to the Catholic Monarchs. Close at hand is the **Alcázar Genil (47),** a 14th-century Moorish palace which is, however, much altered since the time when it belong to the Nasrite sultanas. Like all such palaces, it was also formerly surrounded by gardens and fields.
From here, the visitor can take the Camino de Ronda to La Huerta de San Vicente, once in the outskirts of the city, but now forming part of the most modern sector of Granada. In this park is the **Federico García Lorca House-Museum (48),** where the writer used to reside when resting. The house is now a centre for meetings and other events connected with the life of the great poet of Fuentevaqueros, where Lorca's birthplace was recently opened to the public. The museum contains fascinating personal effects belonging to Federico García Lorca.
Finally, in Avenida Mediterráneo, we come to the **Science Park (49),** the first of its kind in Andalusia. Here are both permanent and temporary exhibition rooms where visitors are invited to learn about the world of science. The facilities also include a planetarium and astronomical observatory.

Federico García Lorca House-Museum, in La Huerta de San Vicente.

Holy Week.

FESTIVITIES AND POPULAR TRADITIONS

Granada's most popular festivities are the Feast of the Cross, (each 3 May), Holy Week, (between March and April) and Corpus Christi (between May and June). During the first, the entire city is filled with flower-laden crosses competing with each other in beauty and originality. This magnificent scene of colour and fragrance is completed, heightening even more the delight of the senses, by many musical performances. For its part, Holy Week is celebrated with great splendour and religious fervour. Particularly impressive are the Procession of El Cristo de los Gitanos («Christ of the Gypsies») which, lit by torches and fires, wends its way up to the Abbey of El Sacromonte, and the gathering of the faithful before the statue of El Cristo de los Favores in the Campo del Príncipe on Good Friday, when Christ is asked for the traditional three favours. Corpus Christi, on the other hand, has more the character of a *Fiesta Mayor,* with celebrations lasting eight

days and including processions, street parties and bullfights. Corpus Christi is announced by a cavalcade accompanied by *cabezudos* («big-heads»), *gigantes* («giants») and bands of music. The next day sees the celebration of the solemn Procession of El Santísimo, and the installation of a fair on the outskirts of the city, with dancing, tapas and excitement till the early hours.
Another impressive event in the calendar of festivities is the Procession of Nuestra Señora de las Angustias. This takes place on the Day of the Virgin, on the last Sunday in September. Moreover, the conquest of Granada is celebrated each 2 January with a procession in historic costume. This civil and religious procession culminates at the Torre de la Vela, where the bell rings out in affirmation of Hispanic unity. According to tradition, those girls who touch the bell will marry within the year.
Finally, mention should be made of more modern festivities, but ones which already enjoy international prestige. Such is the case of the International Festival of Music and Dance, held between June and July, the International Theatre Festival, which takes place in May, and the International Jazz Festival, in November. Flamenco also has deeply-rooted traditions in Granada, and there are a number of clubs in the typical caves of El Sacromonte where *zambras* and Flamenco shows take place every day.

Statue of Nuestra Señora de las Angustias, patron saint of Granada.

Tortilla al Sacromonte.

THE GASTRONOMY OF GRANADA

Influenced by different cultures and by the heterogeneous geography of the province, Granadan gastronomy is as varied as one could wish. There also exists a wide range of subtle variations in the different dishes, according to district, village or even family. This diversity, nevertheless, can be called «Arabic-Andalusian cuisine», as it blends Moorish and Christian specialities, along with other dishes of Jewish origin. Granadan cuisine offers, then, a long list of succulent dishes of which we can only mention a few here: *habas verdes con jamón* (green beans with ham), *tortilla al Sacromonte,* an omelette made from eggs, brain and potato, and *sopa de ajo blanco,* an exquisite white garlic soup, made with ground almonds. Of the many tapas available, visitors are highly recommended to try the excellent ham of Trévelez, whilst the best wines include those from the Alpujarra district, mostly produced at family wineries using artisanal methods. Finally, the sweets and desserts of Granada deserve mention apart due to their excellent quality and variety, particularly those made in convents by the nuns.

ARTS AND CRAFTS

Granada has always, but particularly since Nasrite times, been an eminently commercial city whose artisanal products enjoy enormous prestige. That the rich and varied arts and crafts of Granada are strongly influenced by Moorish traditions there can be no doubt, but there is also an important Renaissance element very much typical to the province. Many craft workshops continue to function in the city. These are for the most part activities maintained by families who pass their skills down from one generation to the next. In carpentry, *taracea* (marquestry) is one of the most genuine local crafts, whilst in pottery we can mention Fajalauza ceramics as one of the most authentic types. The name comes from the ceramists' workshops in the Moorish Fajalauza harbour, and whose models and techniques have changed little over the centuries. Other traditional crafts are the production of objects in copper, iron and brass, as well as leather goods and textiles, with the production of embroidery, tapestries and carpets.

Taracea *(marquestry) is one of the most typical crafts of Granada.*

EXCURSIONS

Granada province contains an exuberant range of magnificent landscapes which have won it as much praise as has the ancient Nasrite capital itself. This geographical variation, sometimes occurring over short distances, ranges from the high peaks of the Sierra Nevada to the Mediterranean coastline, from arid landscapes to rich farming land, from enclaves whose physiognomy has barely changed since ancient times to the tourist resorts of the coast. This diversity is, in turn, determinant in defining the customs and way of understanding life of all the peoples of this rich province.

Just 30 kilometres separate the city of Granada from Pradollano, 2,100 metres above sea level, the town which gives its name to the ski resort of the **Sierra Nevada.** The category of the infrastructure and services at this resort were underlined recently by its hosting of the 1996 World Alpine Ski Championships. It has over 61 km of slopes, distributed amongst 39

pistes and six cross-country routes. But many more activities are also available to visitors to the Sierra Nevada: climbing, hiking, pony trekking or mountain biking, hang-gliding and so on. There is even a golf course nearby.
The ski resort lies at the foot of Mount Veleta. A road, rising to 3,390 metres and one of the highest in Europe, leads to the summit. The Sierra Nevada contains the highest points in the entire geography of the Iberian Peninsula. Three peaks stand out above all: Mount Mulhacén (3,482 metres), Mount Veleta (3,398) and Mount Alacazaba (3,366). These mountains are prolonged in the form of gently rolling foothills. The view from the top is astounding, and on a clear day even the coast of Africa can be made out. The Alpujarra zone, with its terraced slopes and varied vegetation, stretches out towards the Mediterranean, whilst turning our gaze towards the Atlantic we can enjoy a view of sharp mountain peaks with deep precipices and almost vertical slopes.
This entire zone makes up the **Sierra Nevada Nature Reserve,** an area of 170,000 hectares including easternmost point of Almería province and which was declared a Biosphere Reserve by UNESCO in 1986 due to the wealth of flora and

Sierra Nevada ski resort.

Sierra Nevada Nature Reserve: the River Trévelez.

fauna found here. This wealth of life exists here thanks to the enormous differences in altitude, ranging from 400 metres to 3,500 metres above sea level. The outstanding fauna here include the Cabra Montés, mountain goat, whilst the rushing waters of its rivers abound in trout.
To the north of the Sierra Nevada at an altitude of over 1,000 metres stretches a great high plateau in which we find the so-called *Hoyas* of **Guadix** and **Baza.** The road leading to these towns from Granada has been a key element in communications since earliest times, when it was the only accessible link between Eastern and Western Andalusia. For the same reason, these were important enclaves both during Roman and Moorish times. Both are interesting monumental centres. The Moorish baths in Baza, with three rooms, are the oldest in Spain, dating back to the 10th century. **Guadix** is renowned, above all, for its troglodyte site, with cave houses carved out of the rocks and from which all that can be seen from the

exterior are whitewashed walls and chimneys. To enable the visitor to find out more about this type of dwelling, so typical of the district, a cave museum recreates the lifestyle of their inhabitants, as well as displaying examples of local arts and crafts.
From Guadix, the visitor is recommended to approach the Alpujarra region along the beautiful route around the Marquisate of Zenete. A local road takes us to **Jerez del Marquesado.** Its characteristic urban layout tells us clearly that this, like the other towns we shall visit, is of Moorish origin. Next is **Lanteira,** a zone with important deposits of iron which were first mined by the Romans. Of particular beauty, however, are the **Mines of Alquife,** open-cast mines which are still operational. Further on, we come to **Lacalahorra.** Its castle, in Italian Renaissance style, was built in the early-16th century. Well-conserved, it is open to the public and constitutes the town's main attraction. A detour now takes us to **Aldeire,** a fine belvedere over the Marquisate. Back on the road, we continue to Dólar, from where we take the direction of **El Puerto de la Ragua,** an enclave surrounded by magnificent forests which affords incomparable panoramic views over the countryside.

Guadix: cave houses.

Castle and church, Orgiva.

The same road takes us to **La Alpujarra.** Due to the poor communications it suffered until recently, this picturesque region –particularly beautiful is the zone known as the Alpujarra Alta– has survived practically unaltered since Moorish times. The Western, or Granadan Alpujarra ranges from the mountains of the Sierra Nevada down to the sea, the differences in altitude blessing it with a number of microclimates. It enjoys higher rainfall than the Eastern area, in Almería province, which is more arid and less dramatically mountainous. The difficult terrain of the Alpujarra made it the refuge of many Moors after their expulsion had been decreed, making this the last redoubt of Muslim presence on the Peninsula. Now, its beauty and idiosyncrasy have made it an extraordinarily popular area with lovers of rural tourism. In the High Alpujarra, amongst snow and orange groves, perched on the mountain slopes are tiny light-filled villages of whitewashed buildings in the typical cube-like shape, arranged along winding narrow streets. All are of great charm, but we can mention particularly **Trévelez,** the highest, standing 1,476 metres above sea level on the slopes of Mount Mulhacén. This village is well-known for its ham, cured in the cool mountain air. On 5 August each year, the *romería,* pilgrimage, of the Virgen de las Nieves takes place, culminating on the summit of Mount Mulhacén, whilst 13 June, Saint Anthony's day, the wars between the Moors and the Christians are commemorated and recreated in a popular festivity. Between Pampaneira and Capileira we come to the **Poqueira Gully,** which lies between mounts Veleta and Mulhacén, commanding impressive views. In **Capileira** we can visit the Alpujarra Museum to admire the famous *jarapas,* handmade rugs, and local ceramic work. **Bubión** has an ancient artisanal loom and a dried flower workshop. A curiosity is the existence of a Buddhist monastery near **Pampaneira.** Finally, we end our tour at **Orgiva,** the capital of the High Alpujarra. This village contains a fine 16th-century church, and an 18th-century Andalusi-inspired Castle-Palace. A different excursion, a different landscape, is offered by a trip to the coast of Granada. This stretch of coastline between the Costa del Sol of Málaga and the coast of Almería has become known as the **Costa Tropical** in allusion to the local microclimate.

Capileira.

Salobreña.

Here, the looming mountains of the Sierra Nevada protect the zone from the north wind, creating a subtropical microclimate which favours the cultivation of crops found only exceptionally in Europe, such as sugar cane, custard apples and bananas. The coast is dotted with cliffs, coves and broad beaches, dominated by the silhouettes of ancient castles and look-out towers, the defensive line of the different conquerors of the region and strongholds against the frequent pirate attacks the coastline one suffered. Many of these constructions date back to Nasrite times, some built on the site of Phoenician works. Most have been restored and altered at more later dates. The Costa Tropical contains a number of tourist resorts, and whilst some have been transformed by the tourist boom, others have retained much of their original air. Such is the case of **La Herradura,** surrounded by green of a Protected Natural Area, and **Salobreña,** a typical white village in the foothills dominated by a castle originally built by the Phoenicians and which was used by the Nasrite royal family as a summer residence and as a prison for deposed Granadan kings. **Motril** is the most important town and port on the coast of Granada. Its most outstanding monuments include the Collegiate Church of La Encarnación and the Sanctuary of Nuestra Señora de la Cabeza, built on the site of a Moorish palace. **Almuñécar** has also grown into an important seaside resort but, besides its beaches, it also contains such attractions as its Castle, its Archaeological Museum (installed in Roman galleries), and its Bird Park.

A final suggested excursion takes in the zone to the west of Granada. This includes **Santa Fe,** the city-encampment created by the Catholic Monarchs for the final siege of the Nasrite capital; **Fuentevaqueros,** with the birthplace of the poet Federico García Lorca, now a house-museum; **Montefrío,** whose old city perches on a steep rock, crowned by a castle and the village church; **Loja**, declared a national monument, and whose monuments include the Alcazaba, the old Pilgrims' Hospital and the Church of La Encarnación; and **Alhama de Granada,** famed for its Moorish baths, which still function. Nevertheless, the town, which stands on a rocky peak amongst green countryside, also conserves important remains dating back to Roman times.

Almuñécar.

CONTENTS